Ime Your Memory

2nd Edition

By
Ron Fry

CAREER PRESS
180 Fifth Avenue
P.O. Box 34
Hawthorne, NJ 07507
1-800-CAREER-1
201-427-0229 (outside U.S.)
FAX: 201-427-2037

Copyright © 1994 by Ron Fry

IMPROVE YOUR MEMORY (2ND ED.)
ISBN 1-56414-080-6, $6.95
Cover design by A Good Thing, Inc.
Printed in the U.S.A. by Book-mart Press

To order this title by mail, please include price as noted above, $2.50 handling per order, and $1.00 for each book ordered. Send to: Career Press, Inc., 180 Fifth Ave., P.O. Box 34, Hawthorne, NJ 07507.

Or call toll-free 1-800-CAREER-1 (Canada: 201-427-0229) to order using VISA or MasterCard, or for further information on books from Career Press.

Library of Congress Cataloging-in-Publication Data

Fry, Ronald W.
    Improve your memory / by Ron Fry. -- 2nd ed.
        p.   cm.
    Includes index.
    ISBN 1-56414-080-6 : $6.95
    1. Mnemonics. 2. Memory. I. Title.
    BF385.F79   1994
    153.1'4--dc20   94-5485
                                                              CIP

HOW TO STUDY
PROGRAM

How to Study, 3rd Ed. (ISBN 1-56414-075-X, 224 pp., $9.95)

"Ace" Any Test, 2nd Ed. (ISBN 1-56414-079-2, 128 pp., $6.95)

Improve Your Memory, 2nd Ed. (ISBN 1-56414-080-6, 128 pp., $6.95)

Improve Your Reading, 2nd Ed. (ISBN 1-56414-077-6, 128 pp., $6.95)

Manage Your Time, 2nd Ed. (ISBN 1-56414-078-4, 128 pp., $6.95)

Take Notes, 2nd Ed. (ISBN 1-56414-076-8, 128 pp., $6.95)

Write Papers, 2nd Ed. (ISBN 1-56414-081-4, 128 pp., $6.95)

Available individually at your favorite bookstore or as a set by calling 1-800-CAREER-1.

STUDY SMARTER, NOT HARDER!

Ron Fry's* HOW TO STUDY *Program, the best-selling and most acclaimed study series of all time, has sold more than 1,000,000 copies in four years. It is used in colleges, high schools and junior highs and by parents and students throughout the world. And Ron has appeared on hundreds of radio and TV shows and countless newspaper and magazine articles and profiles again and again to trumpet his message: Study Smarter, Not Harder!

Here are just a few of the things reviewers have said about ***Ron Fry's* HOW TO STUDY *Program:***

"These books belong in every secondary library and perhaps in every English classroom. **Highly recommended.**"
— *Library Materials Guide*, Christian Schools International

"Fry's **lively style of writing** makes the book **very useful**."
— *Library Journal*

"Fry has an **appealing, down-to-earth style** that makes this text **accessible and practical.** A regular classroom teacher could extract pertinent lessons to prepare all students to be more successful scholars. The Series would also be appropriate for self-study by college students."
— *Intervention* magazine

"...**approachable, chatty and interactive.** Fry speaks directly to the reader in an **encouraging and sympathetic** fashion it will benefit students from high school age on up."
— *Kliatt Young Adult Paperback Guide*

"...I really liked *How to Study*. **A great gift** for any student."
— *Bookviews*

"**Wow! This guy makes sense, he's funny, and he is easy to read.** I got the feeling this approach might even work for me!"
— Virginia Meldrum, owner of the Owl's Tree bookstore

"This series **could be useful in resource rooms, in a regular classroom setting or as a self-study guide.**"
— Learning Disabilities Association of Canada

Table of

CONTENTS

WHO IS THIS BOOK *REALLY* FOR?

Improve Your Memory was the next-to-last-written (and the last revised) of the six companion volumes added to the original *How to Study.* All were originally written, or so I thought at the time, for high school students. But over the years I've discovered that the students buying these books are either already in college (which says wonderful things about the preparation they got in high school), in junior high (which says something much more positive about their motivation and, probably, eventual success) or returning to college (about whom more later).

Many of you reading this are adults. Some of you are returning to school. And some of you are long out of school but have figured out that if you could learn *now* the study skills your teachers never taught you, you'll do better in your careers.

All too many of you are parents with the same lament: "How do I get Johnny (Janie) to do better in school? He (she) studies like crazy but can't remember anything at test time."

So I want to briefly take the time to address every one of the audiences for this book and discuss some of the factors particular to each of you:

If you're a high school student

You should be particularly comfortable with the format of the book—its relatively short sentences and paragraphs, occasionally humorous (hopefully) headings and subheadings—and the language used. I wrote it with you in mind!

If you're a junior high school student

You are trying to learn how to study at *precisely* the right time. Sixth, seventh and eighth grades—before that sometimes cosmic leap to high school—is without a doubt the period in which all these study skills should be mastered, since doing so will make high school not just easier but a far more positive and successful experience. Although written for high school-level readers, if you're serious enough about studying to be reading this book, I doubt you'll have trouble with the concepts or the language. Since remembering what you study is arguably even more important than studying in the first place, learning these memory techniques *now* will really put you in the catbird's seat. I daresay few of your peers will be able to figure out how you memorized the Periodic Table in one night!

If you're a "traditional" college student...

...somewhere in the 18 to 25 age range, I hope you have already mastered all the study skills covered in my series, and are just perusing this book because finals or the GRE are looming. Even if you've been a mediocre student, learning the many memory techniques covered in this book *must* help you in the years to come, whatever you do.

If you're the parent of a student of any age

You must be convinced of one incontestable fact: It is highly unlikely that your child's school is doing anything to teach him or her how to study. Yes, of course they should. Yes, I know that's what you thought you paid taxes for. Yes, yes, yes. But, but, but—believe me, *they're not doing it*. And I can virtually guarantee that even in schools with great reading programs, teachers who actually teach kids how to take good notes and an afternoon test prep course that prepares them for all the alphabet tests...you won't find *any* specific class to help your student learn how to improve his or her memory.

What does this mean to you? Your involvement in your child's education is absolutely essential to his or her eventual success. Surprisingly enough, the results of every study done in the last two decades about what affects a child's success in school concludes that only one factor *overwhelmingly* affects it, every time: parental involvement. Not the size of the school, the number of language labs, how many of the student body go on to college, how many great teachers there are (or lousy ones). All factors, yes. *But none as significant as the effect you can have.*

So please, take the time to read this book (and all of the others in the series, but especially *How to Study)* yourself. Learn what your kids *should* be learning. (And which of the other five subject-specific books in the Series your child needs the most.)

And you can help tremendously, *even if you were not a great student yourself, even if you never learned great study skills*. You can learn now together with your child—not only will it help him or her in school, it will help *you* on the job, whatever your job. Wouldn't it be nice if you could remember

11

all the due dates of all the projects you're working on without glancing at the calendar? (At which point you probably need to read *Manage Your Time* to make all those deadlines!)

Even if you think you need help only in a single area—or two or three—don't use only the specific book in my program that highlights that subject. Read *How to Study* first, *all the way through*. First of all, it will undoubtedly help you increase your mastery of skills you thought you already had. And it will cover those you need help with in a more concise manner. With that background, you will get *more* out of whichever of the other six books you use.

If you're a nontraditional student

If you're going back to high school, college or graduate school at age 25, 45, 65 or 85—you probably need the help these seven books offer more than anyone! Why? Because the longer you've been out of school, the more likely you don't remember what you've forgotten. And you've forgotten what you're supposed to remember! As much as I emphasize that it's rarely too early to learn good study habits, I must also emphasize that it's never too *late*. And, since our memories tend to slowly deteriorate as we get older (with the notable exception of *memory-meister* Harry Lorayne), this book is probably the one you need most.

Having said that, let me note that you may well have some big adjustments to make. Let's see if I can help make them easier.

Particular problems of nontraditional students

If you're returning to school and attempting to carry even a partial load of courses while simultaneously holding down a job, raising a family or both, there are some particular problems you face that you probably didn't the first time you were in school:

> ***Time and money pressures.*** Let's face it, when all you had to worry about was going to school, it simply *had* to be easier than going to school, raising a family and working for a living simultaneously! (And it was!)

> ***Self-imposed fears of inadequacy.*** You may well convince yourself that you're just "out of practice" with all this school stuff. You don't even remember what color highlighter to use! While some of this fear is valid, most is not. The valid part is that you are returning to an academic atmosphere, one that you may not have even visited for a decade or two. And it *is* different (which I'll discuss more below) than the "work-a-day" world. That's just a matter of adjustment and, trust me, will take a matter of days, if not hours, to dissipate. But I suspect what many of you are really fearing is that you just aren't in that school "mentality" anymore, that you don't "think" the same way. Or, perhaps more pertinently to this book, that the skills you need to succeed in school are rusty.
>
> I think these last fears are groundless. You've been out there thinking and doing for quite a few years, perhaps very successfully, so it's really ridiculous to think school will be so different. It won't be. Relax.
>
> Maybe you're worried because you didn't exactly light up the academic power plant the

first time around. Well, neither did Edison or Einstein or a host of other relatively successful people. Concentrate on how much *more* qualified you are for school *now* than you were *then!*

Feeling you're "out of your element"—This is a slightly different fear, the fear that you just don't fit in any more. After all, you are *not* 18 again. But then, neither are fully half the college students on campus today. That's right, fully 50-percent of all college students are older than 25. The reality is, you'll probably feel more in your element now than you did the first time around!

You'll see teachers differently—Probably a plus. It's doubtful you'll have the same awe you did the first time around. At worst, you'll consider teachers your equals. At best, you'll consider them younger and not necessarily as successful or experienced as you are.

There **are** *differences in academic life.* It's slower than the "real" world, and you may well be moving significantly faster than its normal pace. When you were 18, an afternoon without classes meant a game of Frisbee. Now it might mean catching up on a week's worth of errands, cooking (and freezing) a week's worth of dinners and/or writing four reports due last week. Despite your own hectic schedule, do not expect campus life to accelerate in response. You will have to get used to people and systems with far less interest in speed.

I first wrote ***How to Study*** in 1988, convinced that schools were doing a lousy job of teaching kids how to study—synonymous, to me, with teaching them how to *learn*—and that no one was picking up the slack. (I was also convinced—and still am—that most kids wanted *desperately* to learn but would, without some help, find it easier to fail. And failure, once welcomed, is a nasty habit to break.)

Published in 1989, most bookstores wedged one or two copies of ***Study*** in between the hundreds of phone book-sized test prep volumes. Career Press wasn't a big enough publisher to convince the "chains"—Waldenbooks, Barnes & Noble, B. Dalton—to stock it in any quantity or rich enough to spend any money promoting it.

Nevertheless, tens of thousands of people who obviously needed ***How to Study*** ferreted out copies wherever they lurked and bought them. In 1990, the chains—who *are* smart enough to at least spot a winner the *second* time around—bought 6-copy "prepacks" and gave the book a little more prominence. (Meaning you didn't have to get a hernia removing other books to find a copy of ***Study***.) Career Press sent me around the country to appear on radio and TV, including CNN. And hundreds of newspapers and magazines noticed what we were doing and started writing about ***How to Study***. (The fact that test scores had declined for the hundred-fortieth year in a row or so probably had something to do with this, but who am I to quibble with the attention?)

In 1991, *booksellers* started calling to say they hoped I was planning some follow-up books to ***Study***. And hundreds of parents and students wrote or called to indicate they needed more help in some specific areas. ***Ron Fry's* HOW TO STUDY *Program*** was born, featuring a second edition of ***Study*** and four new books—***Improve Your Reading, Manage***

Your Time, Take Notes and Write Papers—that delved even deeper into critical study skills. That year I spent more time on the phone doing radio shows than I did, I think, with my wife and 2-year-old daughter.

In 1992, I added two more volumes—*"Ace" Any Test* and **Improve Your Memory**, both of which were pretty much written in response to readers' letters. These two books quickly became the second- and third-biggest sellers of the seven in the series, beaten only by **How to Study.** Evidently, my readers knew darned well what they were requesting.

By the way, in both 1992 and 1993, I added mightily to my Frequent Flyer accounts while talking to people nationwide about studying. I wound up visiting 50 cities, some twice, and appearing on more TV and radio shows than are listed in your daily newspaper.

The result of all this travel was twofold: First, sales of all seven books have skyrocketed, in part because of the chance I've been given to talk about them on so many shows and in so many newspapers and magazines. Second, I got to meet and talk with tens of thousands of students and parents, many of whom confirmed the ongoing need for these books *because very little has changed since I first wrote* **How to Study** *some six years ago.*

Test scores of every kind are lower today than they were then. More and more students are dropping out or, if they *do* manage to graduate high school, are finding they are not equipped to do *any*thing, whether they're hoping to go to college or trying to land a job. And more and more parents are frustrated by their children's inability to learn and their schools' seeming inability to teach.

With so much new feedback, it was time to revise all seven books, all of which are being published in time for "back to school" in 1994. In every book, I've included additional topics and expanded on others. I've changed some examples, simplified some, eliminated some. I've rewritten sentences, paragraphs or entire sections that students seemed to be struggling with. Most importantly, I've tried to reflect my new understanding of just who is reading these books—"traditional" students, their parents *and* nontraditional (i.e. older) students, many of those self-same parents—and write in such a way to include all three audiences.

A couple of caveats

Before we get on with all the tips and techniques you need to remember more of what you read and study, let me make two important points about all seven study books.

First, I believe in gender equality, in writing as well as in life. Unfortunately, I find constructions such as "he and she," "s/he," "womyn" and the like painfully awkward. I have therefore attempted to sprinkle pronouns of both genders throughout the text. Some teachers, for example, are "he," some are "she." I think this is preferable to using the masculine pronoun throughout but proclaiming one's feminist leanings or to creating so-called "gender-neutral" words or phrases that I find inhibit the "flow" I try to achieve in my writing.

Second, you will find many pieces of advice, examples, lists and other words, phrases and sections spread throughout two or more of the seven books. Certainly *How to Study*, which is an overview of all the study skills, necessarily contains, though in summarized form, some of each of the other six books. But there are discussions of note-taking in *Write Papers* and *Take Notes*, tips about essay tests in *"Ace" Any Test* and *Write Papers*, time management techniques in *Manage Your Time* and *Improve Your Reading*.

The repetition is unavoidable. While I urge everyone to read all seven books in the series, but especially *How to Study*, they *are* seven individual books. And many people only buy one of them. Consequently, I must include in each the pertinent material *for that topic*, even if that material is then repeated in a second or even a third book. As I will point out again and again throughout all the books, these study skills are intimately interrelated. You can't discuss writing papers without covering taking notes for those papers. Or improving your reading without discussing how to take notes from textbooks or how to remember what you've just read.

In many cases, not only is the same topic covered, but it is covered in the same language or uses the same example. If I am particularly happy with the way I covered a subject in one book, I have not gone out of my way to completely rewrite a sentence, paragraph or, for that matter, a whole section just to say it "differently" in another. (Besides, for those who follow my advice and work with all seven books, I think the repetition of some of the same important points can only help them learn it more quickly and easily.)

That said, I can guarantee that the nearly 1,000 pages of my **HOW TO STUDY Program** contain the most wide-ranging, comprehensive and complete system of studying ever published. I have attempted to create a system that is usable, that is useful, that is practical, that is learnable. One that *you* can use—whatever your age, whatever your level of achievement, whatever your IQ—to start doing better in school *immediately*.

I hope after reading these books you'll agree I've succeeded.

I'm sure after reading these books that *you'll* succeed.

Ron Fry
May, 1994

THANKS FOR THE MEMORIES

Let me tell you about my good friend Tony Rutigliano, possibly the paradigm for Jerry Lewis's "Absent-Minded Professor." The Tonester would walk through the house with his glasses on top of his head, asking everyone if they had seen them. On any household project he tackled, he'd spend as much time looking for tools he'd put down as sawing wood, drilling holes or hammering nails. And, of course, I always offered to drive whenever we planned to go off somewhere. If I waited for Tony to remember where he'd put his keys, I'd still be cooling my heels.

Tony, who has been invaluable as editor, critic and general sounding board on many of my books (and is the very successful and highly respected publisher of *Sales & Marketing Management* magazine) asked if we couldn't do a memory book that would solve his problems. The result—the first edition of **Improve Your Memory**, published in 1992—was incredibly popular, indicating, to me at least, that there are a lot of "Tony's" out there who just can't remember everything they need to.

Improve Your Memory

This new edition is even more complete—a simple, practical, easy-to-use memory book that will help you:

Remember numbers

Remember dates and facts

Retain more of what you read the *first* time you read it

Take notes that will help you score well on tests and term papers

Remember numbers

Build a bigger vocabulary

Remember how to spell

Remember names and faces

Remember numbers (get the feeling this is *every*one's biggest problem!?)

What's more, **Improve Your Memory** will help you do *all* of this without a mind-numbing amount of time and effort. Its advice is easy to learn, even easier to apply.

And, along the way, you might even develop skills for knowing at all times where you've left your car keys and wallet...or glasses, for that matter

The best way to approach this book is to read Chapters 1 through 10 straight through, then go back and review some of the mechanics of memory improvement contained in Chapters 3 through 10. (And if you have ADD—or are the parent of someone who does—be sure to read the brand-new Chapter 11 that deals specifically with this expanding problem.)

After this review, take the test in Chapter 12 and see how much you've improved *your* memory. I'm sure you'll be amazed. When you've finished this book, you'll be effortlessly flexing mental muscles you never knew you had!

Chapter One

IT'S ALL IN THE MIND

As the future writer of **Lolita**, Vladimir Nabakov, escaped war-torn Europe with his wife and son in May, 1940, he enjoyed an incredible moment. Walking toward the dock with young Dmitri, he knew that the boy would remember for the rest of his life the first time he saw the tall smokestacks of the ocean liner. As Nabakov's biographer Brian Boyd notes, "He always considered that to recognize a future recollection at the moment it happened, to know with certainty that *this* particular moment would later be recalled, was somehow to cheat the tyranny of time."

That, after all, is the essence of memory: a conquest of time, an ability to experience, to get in touch with some fact or sensation *as if it had just happened*. Developing a skilled or practiced memory is to keep facts, formulas and experiences at your disposal so that you can use them when you need to or want to...when*ever* you need or want.

How could Nabakov recognize such moments? What made them stand out?

Well, what makes something memorable is its *extra*ordinariness, the amount that it stands *out* from our usual experiences.

The reason so many of us forget where we put the car keys or our eyeglasses is that putting these objects down is the most ordinary of occurrences, part and parcel of the most humdrum aspects of our lives. We have trouble remembering facts and formulas from books and classroom lectures for the same reason. To be schooled is to be bombarded with facts day in and day out. How do you make those facts memorable? (And, by the way, has anyone seen my glasses?)

You can call me Hal

In order to understand how to make the important facts memorable, how to keep them stored safely at least until final exams, let's first take a look at how the brain and, more specifically, memory work.

I'm going to call upon a rather useful, and for that reason somewhat overused analogy and ask you to think of your brain as that computer you typed your last term paper on—an organic computer, wired with nerves, hooked up to various INPUT devices (your five senses), and possessed of both ROM (read-only memory) and RAM (random access memory).

The ROM is the data you can't touch—the disk-operating system, the information that tells your heart to pump and your lungs to breathe.

On the other hand, RAM is much more accessible. Like most PCs nowadays, your brain stores RAM in two places: *short-term* memory (think of that old single-sided, low-density floppy disk you've been meaning to get rid of) and *long-term* memory (that one-gigabyte baby of a hard drive).

OK, so what happens to INPUT in this system?

A matter of choice

Well, given the bombardment of data we receive every day, our brains constantly are making choices. Data either goes in one ear and out the other, or it stops in short-term memory. But when that old floppy disk gets full, the brain is left with a choice—jettison some old information or pass it on to the hard drive.

How does it make a decision *which* information to pass on and *where* to store it?

Well, scientists aren't positive about this yet, but, of course, they have theories.

The most readily stored and accessed is data that's been *rehearsed*—gone over again and again. Most of us readily access our knowledge of how to read, how to drive, the year Columbus "discovered" America, the name of the first president of the United States and other basics without any difficulty at all. (At worst, you remember "Columbus sailed the ocean blue in 1492.") We've worn familiar paths through our memory banks accessing this type of information or skill.

Why, then, can some people recite the names, symbols and atomic weights of the elements of the Periodic Table—while they're playing (and winning) *Trivial Pursuit*—as easily as they can the date of Columbus's dubious achievement?

To return to our computer analogy, this information has gotten "tagged" or "coded" in some way so that it can be easily retrieved. For instance, before storing a file in your computer's long-term RAM, you give it a name, one that will easily conjure what exactly that file is. In other words, you make the file *stand out* in some way from the host of other files you've stored on your disk drive.

For some people, myriad bits of data are almost auto-matically tagged so that they can be quite easily and handily stored and retrieved. But most of us, if we are to have exceptional memories, must make a special effort.

Woe unto the poor memorizer

Students, of course, must possess or develop good memories or they risk mediocrity or failure. The mere act of getting by in school means remembering a lot of dates, mathematical and scientific formulas, historical events, characters and plots, some-times entire poems. (I had a whacko biology teacher who made us memorize the 52 parts of a frog's body, which, of course, has been absolutely essential to my subsequent career success. Not.)

Practically, there are two ways of going about this. The most familiar way is rehearsal or repetition. By any name, it is the dull process of reading or pronouncing something over and over until you have it "by heart." (I really didn't want to hold the 52 parts of a frog *too* close to my heart, though.)

But a much easier way—getting back to our computer analogy—is to tag or code things we are trying to remember. And to do so with images and words that are either outrageous or very familiar.

For instance, have you ever wondered how, in the days before index cards, ballpoint pens or teleprompters troubadours memorized song cycles and politicians memorized lengthy speeches? Well, in the case of the great Roman orator Cicero, it was a matter of associating the parts of his speeches with the most familiar objects in his life—the rooms of his home. Per-haps the opening of a speech would be linked to his bed cham-ber, the next part to his yard. As he progressed through the speech, he would, in essence, mentally take his usual morning stroll passing through the rooms of his home.

In other cases, more outrageous associations work much better. (And the more outrageous, ridiculous or impossible the association, the *more* memorable it is.) Let's take an example. Although absent-mindedness is not one of the problems we will try to solve in this book, a common cure for it illustrates my point.

If you frequently have trouble remembering, say, where you put down your pen, get into the habit of conjuring up some startling image *linking* (a key word later on in this book) the pen and the place. For example, as you're putting your pen down on the kitchen table, think about eating peas off a plate with it or of the pen sticking straight up in a pile of mashed potatoes. Even days later, when you think, "Hmm, where did I leave that ballpoint?" the peas and plate (or mashed potatoes) will come to mind, reminding you of the kitchen table.

By the way, this is an easy habit to get into. It's helped me cut down on swearing and has saved me a lot of money on string!

The rest is easy

These are the essential principles of memory for which the computer analogy is particularly apt. After all, when dealing with the mind, as with the machine, the GIGO (garbage in, garbage out) rule applies. If you passively allow your brain's process to decide what and how items are stored, you will have a jumbled memory, from which it is difficult to extract even essential bits of knowledge.

On the other hand, if you are selective and careful about assigning useful tags to the items headed for the long-term memory banks, you are on the way to being able to memorize the Manhattan telephone directory!

If you have trouble remembering your *own* phone number, I would run, not walk, to the next chapter.

Chapter Two

AND NOW FOR A LITTLE QUIZ

I know what you're thinking. You bought this book so you could improve your memory and perform better on exams and those darned pop quizzes, and now I turn around and throw some *more* tests your way. I could note that "them's the breaks!"

Or, as one of my high school teachers used to say, I could encourage you to think of tests as your best friends. In this book, and throughout your academic career, tests will give you the measure of how far you've come...and how far you've got to go. Follow the advice in this book and your score on similar tests in the last chapter should be 25 percent higher.

Test 1: Numbers

Look at the number below this paragraph for no more than 10 seconds. Then cover the page (or, better yet, close the book) and write down as much of it—in order—as you can.

275345546086534897

Test 2: Words & Definitions

Below are 15 relatively obscure words along with their definitions. Study this list for 60 seconds. Then cover it up and take the test directly below the list. Allow yourself no more than 90 seconds to complete the quiz...and no peeking.

Crambo	A game in which one person or side must find a rhyme to a word or verse given by another
Rutile	A common reddish-brown mineral (titanium dioxide) with a brilliant metallic luster
Macaronic	Composed of a mixture of languages
Febrific	Producing or marked by fever
Saltando	Playing each note on a stringed instrument staccato by bouncing the bow on the strings
Reechy	Smoky or sooty
Iiwi	A Hawaiian honeycreeper with a red body, black wings and deeply curved red bill
Keelage	A toll on a merchant ship entering a port
Babiche	A rawhide thong, thread or lacings used for making snowshoes
Zuccheto	A small, round skullcap worn by Roman Catholic ecclesiastics
Ukase	Any order or proclamation by an arbitrary or absolute authority
Rivel	A small dumpling made of batter and cooked in broth
Glinn	A bright glow in the sky close to the horizon

Improve Your Memory

Pomace   The residue from apples or other fruit after crushing and pressing

Dene   A bare sandy tract near the sea

Have you studied the words diligently? OK, no cheating now, fill in the blanks:

1. What would you use to make apple cider? _____.

2. You could both insult and impress your chain-smoking friend by calling her _____.

3. A priest's _____ is black, a bishop's violet.

4. Something composed of a mixture of languages is called _____.

5. If you needed to make snowshoes, you'd use _____.

6. Once you made the snowshoes and were ready for some soup, you'd drop the _____ right in.

7. The doctor declared my husband was _____

8. Well, I didn't find any gold, but I mined some _____.

9. The composition was notoriously difficult, requiring the whole middle section be played _____.

10. Despite its name, the red-billed _____ is not creepy.

11. OK, poker, gin or _____?

12. The ship's captain wasn't surprised at the high _____ he had to pay.

13. Ukase does not mean "your house" (as in, "my casa is ukasa, baby"). It means: _____

14. Where would you see a glinn? _____

15. And if a dene were nearby, where would be probably be? _____

Test 3: Names

Give yourself three minutes to memorize the names of the President/Vice-President combinations below:

> Thomas Jefferson / George Clinton
> James Madison / Elbridge Gerry
> James Monroe / Daniel Tompkins
> John Quincy Adams / John C. Calhoun
> Andrew Jackson / Martin Van Buren
> Martin Van Buren / Richard Johnson
> James Polk / George Dallas
> Franklin Roosevelt / John Garner
> Franklin Roosevelt / Henry Wallace
> Franklin Roosevelt / Harry Truman
> Harry Truman / Alben Barkley
> Lyndon Johnson / Hubert Humphrey

Time's up! OK, cover the list and fill in as many of the blanks as you can. If you get last names only, that's fine, but consider first names "extra credit." Take another three minutes to complete the quiz:

1. James Madison _____

2. Thomas Jefferson _____

3. Franklin Roosevelt:_____

_____

_____

4. James Monroe _____

5. John Q. Adams _____

6. _____ John Calhoun

7. James Polk _____

8. Harry Truman _____

9. Lyndon Johnson _____

10. _____Henry Wallace

Test 4: Dates

Here are the dates of 10 historical events. Take up to three minutes to memorize them, then cover the list and take the quiz on the next page.

1948   Israel is officially recognized as a state by U.S. President Harry Truman.

1876   Custer is defeated at Little Big Horn.

1791   Mozart is born.

1606   England founds the Jamestown colony in Virginia.

1494   Leonardo da Vinci begins working on "The Last Supper."

1912   Woodrow Wilson is elected to his first term as President of the United States.

1947   Great Britain grants independence to India.

1812   Charles Dickens is born.

1519   Cortez invades Mexico City.

1564   William Shakespeare is born.

1. The British founded Jamestown in _____.

2. William Shakespeare was born in _____.

3. Custer had is last stand in 18_____.

4. We celebrated the 200th year of Mozart's birth in
   _____.

5. India became independent on Jan. 1, _____.

6. The Spaniards invaded Mexico City in _____.

7. Israel became a nation in _____.

8. Charles Dickens was born in _____.

9. Woodrow Wilson was elected to his first term in
   _____.

10. Leonardo da Vinci began work on "The Last
    Supper," perhaps his best-known work, in _____.

Test 5: Reading Retention

Read the text below, then answer the questions following. Give yourself two minutes to read the text and two minutes to answer the questions *without referring to the paragraph*!

Franklin Delano Roosevelt's chief accomplishments encompass both domestic and international activities. First elected when the country suffered a severe economic collapse, he was instrumental in mobilizing the nation's people and resources to spearhead a recovery.

In present-day economic terms, he presided over the greatest turnaround in the nation's history.

Applying the full weight of central government, he established the principle of government as the court of last resort. Specifically, this welfare approach included: the establishment of Social Security, a variety of projects that created millions of jobs, federally guaranteed insurance on depositor's bank accounts, stock market regulation, rural power and electrification, the establishment of minimum wage and working-conditions standards, and unemployment insurance.

During World War II, FDR presided over the largest military buildup and subsequent engagement ever faced by the United Sates. He was the successful commander in chief directing the military forces of the nation in a global encounter with the forces of Fascism and expansionism.

Roosevelt, early on, recognized the threat that the Axis powers presented and mobilized the country primarily by helping to arm England via the mechanism of Lend-Lease against them. There were those, and many in high places, who sought to minimize the American role in the impending war. Roosevelt, however, was accurate in his belief in the inevitability of U.S. involvement. He recognized the ultimate threat to American freedom that Fascism represented. When the Japanese attack on Pearl Harbor was a *fait accompli*, Roosevelt was ready.

Roosevelt's wartime stewardship demonstrated, as it had during the Great Depression, his genius for leadership. His words mobilized the nation. His efforts, together with those of Churchill and Stalin, led the free world to victory.

Some revisionist historians would argue that post-war activities (begun at the Yalta Conference) jeopardized America's postwar influence, particularly in Eastern Europe. It seems more logical to assume that the Cold War rivalry that existed between the U.S. and the U.S.S.R. was a natural outgrowth of two antithetical systems, each feeling heady with victory, each determined to make their manner of governing the law of the entire world.

Roosevelt's place in history is assured. Although himself privileged by birth, he displayed an unusual compassion for the average man. A noncombatant because of his illness, he demonstrated a courage and leadership that stood as a fine example for battlefield troops.

Questions

1. The writer's main purpose in this selection is to:
   A. Describe world conditions during FDR's presidency.
   B. Demonstrate Roosevelt's grasp of both domestic and international problems.
   C. Indicate that leadership is essential for an effective presidency.
   D. Indicate the broad scope of programs developed to reinvigorate a depressed economy.
   E. Emphasize the inevitability of confrontation between countries with different forms of government.

2. The author asserts that Roosevelt:
   A. Provided necessary leadership in turning the economy around.
   B. Did not hesitate to involve government.

  C. Was the grandfather of the welfare state.

  D. Pioneered many social reforms and make-work programs.

  E. All of the above

3. One can conclude that Roosevelt:

  A. Understood the real threat posed by Fascism.

  B. Was able to marshal the necessary cooperation among allies for the conduct of a successful global war effort.

  C. Understood the necessity to arm England.

  D. Was not anxious for war but realistic about its possibility.

  E. All of the above.

4. The phrase "postwar influence" refers directly to:

  A. Agreement on spheres of power determined at Yalta.

  B. An acknowledgment of the military realities when hostilities ceased.

  C. The recognition of the competing natures of Democracy and Communism.

  D. A permanent division of the world along super-power lines.

  E. None of the above.

Here's another chance with some more recent history.

The bickering that has gone on among both white and black South African dissidents, primarily over whether to boycott that country's first free elections, is reminiscent of the playground squabbles we went through as children.

Bosom buddies one moment, down-in-the-dirt antagonists the next, back in class again minutes later.

Is such bickering merely a method of negotiation, a way for each of the sides, but primarily the African National Congress and the Zulu nationalists, to convince the other that unless their demands are met, they may well scuttle the entire process? Again, is it not like the child who, denied the field at first base, takes his ball and goes home, allowing pride to overcome his desire to play ball, no matter what position he is given?

Perhaps, but the real passions that lie behind such brinkmanship cannot be denied. And neither can the very real sense that for many of the "players," there is far more emotion at work than political maneuvering or logic.

Most of the citizenry is tired of the daily deadlines, the factionalism, the ever-changing alliances, enemies turning into friends overnight, friends waking up enemies. Breakthroughs are announced in newspapers' morning editions only to be proved false by the evening.

This disarray has in many cases overshadowed the active campaigning by Nelson Mandela's African National Congress and President F. W. de Klerk's National Party, the two major factions in the election. Their campaign has been further eroded by the party that has, so far at least, opted out of the elections altogether—the Zulu nationalists' Inkatha Freedom Party. It is unthinkable that they and their mercurial leader,

Mangosuthu G. Buthelezi, will hold themselves out of the election process entirely. They simply have too much to lose—patronage, credibility and the ability to incorporate their own platform in the newly formed government—to boycott the elections entirely.

But Buthelezi and his party have defied logic and done the unthinkable before. While many observers believe his holdout to be a shrewd strategic move, one that will enable him to extract every possible concession before he enters the electoral fray, others remember his withdrawal from negotiations last year that many feel would have enabled him to displace de Klerk as the titular opposition leader and expand his influence beyond the predominantly Zulu province of Natal. Instead, he became even more insular and isolated, scared off many former supporters and lost the votes of many who were ready to make him the alternative to Mandela and the ANC.

Questions

1. The author believes the Inkatha Freedom Party:
   A. Can be a viable alternative to the ANC for voters
   B. Cannot afford to boycott the election process
   C. Is ready to expand beyond Natal province
   D. Should depose its leader
2. It is obvious from this reading that:
   A. It's not important who wins the game but how you play that counts

    B. Violence will continue long after the elections are over

    C. Emotions are playing as important or more important a role in South Africa's elections that political logic

    D. F. W. de Klerk cannot win a majority of the votes in this election

3. The writer's purpose in this selection is to:

    A. Discuss the current political situation in South Africa

    B. Analyze the position of the Inkatha Freedom Party

    C. Describe the bickering between the political parties

    D. All of the above

4. The writer thinks the winner of the election will be:

    A. F. W. de Klerk and the National Party

    B. Nelson Mandela and the African National Congress

    C. Inkatha Freedom Party

    D. None of the above

To check how you did on these last two reading selections, see the answers at the very bottom of page 38. (You can go back and check the book itself to figure out the answers to the others.)

How did you do?

Take a piece of paper and write down the scores you got on each of these exercises. This will indicate how much improvement you must do to have a good head for the material you learn in school. It will also provide a benchmark so that you can see how far you've come when you take the similar quizzes in the last chapter.

The emphasis of these five tests was not arbitrary. It corresponds exactly with the skills you will be learning throughout this book: memorizing chains of information (such as the president/vice president and the date/event pairings); developing a sense for numbers; remembering what you read; and getting a better grasp on vocabulary.

ANSWERS TO TEST FIVE
1) B; 2) E; 3) E; 4) A; 1) B; 2) C; 3) D; 4) D

Chapter Three

IT'S TIME TO GET CRAZY

In Chapter 1 we talked about the need to establish tags or codes for items we wish to remember so that our minds will have relatively little difficulty retrieving them from long-term memory.

In this chapter, we will begin talking about one of the methods used for "tagging" items *before they enter* that morass of memory.

The "chain link" method will help you remember items that appear in sequence, whether it's the association of a date with an event, a scientific term with its meaning, or other facts or objects that are supposed to "go together."

The basis for the chain-link system is that memory works best when you associate the unfamiliar with the familiar, though sometimes the association may be a very odd one. But to really make it effective, the odder the better.

Let's get personal

For instance, let's say that I was a literature major who wanted to remember that our friend from Chapter 1, Vladimir Nabakov, published *Lolita,* his most famous novel, in 1958.

The usual way for me to do this would be to repeat over and over again, "*Lolita*, 1958, *Lolita*, 1958, ..." *ad nauseam.* How much easier it would be to just say, "Lolita was my date in '58"! I've established a link between Lolita, the coquettish girl of Nabakov's novel, the date of publication, and some imaginary Saturday night special date. (You'll learn more about how to remember dates in Chapter 8).

In addition, I was able to use another terrific memory technique—rhyming. Rhyme schemes, no matter how silly or banal, can help us remember things for years. For instance, who can forget that it's "*i* before *e* except after *c*, or when it sounds like *a* as in *neighbor* and *weigh*"?

The stranger the better

Or let's step away from schoolwork for a moment to consider the case of a woman who can't remember where she lays anything—car keys, wallet, her month-old baby (just kidding!).

Using the chain-link method would ensure that she would never forget. For instance, let's say she puts her car keys down on her kitchen counter and, as she does, thinks of a car plowing right into the kitchen and through the countertop. Will that woman be able to forget what she did with her keys? Would you?

Or, to pick an example more germane to academic life, let's say that you wanted to remember that *mitosis* is the process whereby one cell divides itself into two. Instead of repeating word and definition countless times, why not think, "My toes is dividing" and form a mental picture of two of your toes separating? Much easier, isn't it?

Soup bone's connected to the...

The best way to teach this technique is by example, so let's take another one. Suppose you wanted to remember the names of the groups of bones and individual bones extending from your fingertips right on up your arm to your collar bone.

They are: phalanges (fingers), metacarpals (palm), carpus (wrist), ulna (inside bone of forearm), radius (outside bone of forearm), olecranon (elbow), humerus (upper arm), clavicle (collar bone).

OK, why don't you study this, cover up the page, and try to recite the names of the bones in order. Take about three minutes to bone up on the list. (I must have my occasional little jokes—they remind me where I am.)

Time's up

How did you do? Did you get them all right? How long do you think you'd have to study this list to be able to recite it perfectly? What if you had to remember all the bones in the human body, all 206 of them? I guarantee you it would take a lot less time were you to establish a chain link that you could instantly retrieve from your memory bank.

Let's go back to our finger and arm example and make this list a bit more amusing:

Phalanges will now become "fall angels." You will think of autumn leaves clutched in your *fingers* turning into angels.

Metacarpals will now be "met car pals." You will think of shaking *hands* with people sitting in a car.

41

Carpus will now be (you guessed it, I hope) "car puss." You will think of looking at your *wrist*watch and seeing in the crystal the face (or *puss*) of a car. Or perhaps you could imagine the car turning into a giant pussy cat. Please, don't let me fantasize for you!

Ulna\radius will now be "my radiant Aunt Ulna."

Olecranon will now be "old crane." And you'll think of the Gershwin song "My Ole Crane." (That's "flame," of course. Sorry, George). Since the *elbow* is also called the "funny bone," you'll think of singing "My Old Crane" and laughing your head off.

Humerus, since it's connected to the *funny bone*, will become "humor us." You'll think of a bunch of very serious people listening to your rendition of "My Ole Crane" and not laughing a bit.

Clavicle becomes "claycicle," and you'll picture a (frozen) piece of Mr. Bill (or Gumby) hanging from your collar. (If you're afraid you'll forget the "v" sound in clavicle, picture his two arms hanging down...forming, of course, a "v"!)

I can just hear you, my gentle readers, saying, "What the heck are we supposed to do with this ridiculous string of associations?...or less polite words to that effect.

Well, now you're supposed to *link* them together into the chain of facts you have to remember for that anatomy final. Here's how you might do it:

> After I saw the *fall angels*, I *met* my *car pals*. I looked at my watch and saw a *car puss* and remembered that I had to meet my *radiant* Aunt *Ulna*. She asked me to sing '*My Ole Crane*,' but her friends said, 'That doesn't *humor us*.' I

tugged at my tie, but it was stuck to the *claycicle* in my collar.

Is this efficient?

You're probably wondering just how much time it took me to construct these ridiculous associations and the even more bizarre story to go with them. The answer: about one minute. I'll bet it will take you a lot longer to memorize the list of arm and hand bones. And my way of doing this is so much more fun! Not only that, but I'd be willing to bet that you'll remember "radiant Aunt Ulna" a lot longer than ulna and radius.

The reason is that you use so much more of your brain when you employ techniques like this. Reciting a list of facts over and over to yourself uses only three of your faculties—sight (as you read them from the page), speech, and hearing—in carving the memory trail. Constructing a bizarre story like the one about the bones also puts to work your imagination, perhaps the most powerful of your mind's many powers.

How the French do it

Let's try another example, one with which I doubt you are at all familiar—the French Revolutionary calendar: Brumaire, Floréal, Frimaire, Fructidore, Germinal, Messidor, Nivôse, Pluviôse, Prairiel, Thermidor, Vendémiaire, Ventôse.

Here's the way I would remember: There'd be a big *broom* sweeping through the *air* across a field of *flowers*. That's the first picture—two down (Brumaire, Floréal).

Now the broom would turn into a *frying pan* flying through the *air* (Frimaire).

Suddenly a refrigerator (naturally, a *Frigidaire)* would open (Fructidore) and out would pop my old friends *Germ and Al*

(Germinal). They'd yell at me, "Hey, why have you got such a *messy door*? (Messidor)

Well, people yelling at me makes me *nervous* (Nivôse) so I'd stammer, "*Pl*ease, *you've toas*ted me." (Pluviôse)

So I got down on some *rail*road tracks to *pray* (Prairiel) until a giant Lobster *Thermidor* came tumbling down in a *vend*ing machine, right out of the *air*. (Vendémaire).

The smell *went* right to my *nose*.

Immediately after making up this story, I turned away from the computer and, without even trying, recited the words I was supposed to have just memorized. It's that easy.

Now you try. How would you remember another obscure list, like this longer one of alphabets? Chalcidian, cuneiform, Cyrillic, devanagari, entrangelo, futhark, Glagol, Glossic, Greek, Gurmukhi, hieroglyphs, hiragana, ideograph, kana, katakana, Kuffic, linear A, linear B, logograph, nagari, naskhi, ogham, pictograph, Roman, runic, syllabary.

Time yourself. When you can construct a series of pictures to remember a list like this—and remember it—all in less than five minutes, you are well on your way to mastering this powerful memory technique.

Hear my song

Observations of people who have been in accidents or suffered other types of severe brain trauma have yielded many interesting insights into the ways our minds and memories work. For instance, people who have had the left side of their brains damaged might lose their ability to speak and remember words and facts, but often are still able to sing songs perfectly.

Current thinking on this is that the faculty for speech resides in the left hemisphere of the brain, while the ability to sing can be found in the right.

Since it is my feeling that the more of your mind's power you put behind the job of remembering, the better you'll do, I'd like to suggest song as another great way to remember strings of information.

For instance, I remember few things from chemistry class in my junior year of high school (not having had memory training at that time). But the one thing I'll never forget is that ionization is a dissociative reaction, that is, it is the result of electrons becoming separated from their nuclei.

The reason I remember this is that Mr. Scott, my crazy chemistry teacher, came into class singing (to the main theme from the opera "Grenada") "I-, I-, I-onization. I-, I-, I-onization. Oh, this is, oh, this is a dissociative reaction in chemistry."

Or, there's the case of one of Robert Frost's most loved poems, "Stopping by Woods on a Snowy Evening."

Did you ever realize that you could sing the entire poem to the music of "Hernando's Hideaway" by Xavier Cugat?

Try it with the last four lines—"The woods are lovely dark and deep, but I have promises to keep, and miles to go before I sleep. And miles to go before I sleep."

And trust me: It works for the whole poem.

Unfortunately, that beautiful poem, one of my favorites, may now be ruined for you forever!

Just do it

My point here is that music is one of the ways that you can create a chain link to improve your memory. As the example of the hand and arm bones above demonstrates, there are many others:

Unusual   To the extent possible, make the chain-link
                 scenarios you construct highly unusual.

45

Active	Don't think of an object just sitting there. Have it do something! Remember Mom and her car smashing through the kitchen counter earlier in the chapter? How can such an image be forgotten?
Emotional	Conjure up a scenario in establishing your chain link that elicits an emotional reaction—joy, sorrow, physical pain, whatever.
Rhyming	Many lessons for preschoolers and those just in first- and second-grade are done with rhymes. If it works for them, it should work for you, right?
Acronyms	If you've taken trigonometry, you've probably come across good old Chief **SOH-CAH-TOA**. If you've been lucky enough to evade trig (or didn't have Mr. Oldehoff in 7th Grade), you've missed one of the easiest way to remember trigonometric functions: **S**ine equals **O**pposite/**H**ypotenuse; **C**osine equals **A**djacent/**H**ypotenuse; **T**angent equals **O**pposite/**A**djacent.

Relax and have fun

You're probably thinking that all of this doesn't sound like it will make your life any easier. I know it *seems* like a lot of work to think of the soundalikes and then construct crazy scenarios or songs using them. Trust me: If you start applying these tips *routinely* as you study, they will quickly become second nature and make you a more efficient student.

Let's try it again

I'm going to give you another set of bones, this time those extending from your toes to your hip. (After the alphabets, this one should be a piece of cake!) They are: phalanges (toes), metatarsals (the foot), tarsus (instep), talus (ankle), fibula (calf), tibia (shin), patella (kneecap), femur (thigh).

Take two minutes to construct a chain link. Then, you know the drill, cover up the paragraph above and recite the bones and bone groups in order.

How'd you do?

Was it easier for you to get to know your bones this time? Were you successful in constructing an easy-to-remember chain link?

Let me take you through the way I might construct such a chain were I to take Anatomy 101 again (perish the thought!):

Phalanges:	Fall (or fell)angels
Metatarsals:	Metal tar pails
Tarsus:	Tarred us
Talus	Tall us
Fibula:	Fabulous
Tibia:	Tubular
Patella:	Fat Ella
Femur:	Fell more

My brief chain-link paragraph would go something like this:

The *angels fell* into the *metal tar pails*. They were *tall*er than *us* and *tarred us* in a *tubular, fabulous* way. *Fat Ella fell more* times than we did.

...ere's the rub

The only problem with this method is that you might occasionally have trouble remembering what your sound-alike signified in the first place (and you don't want to write down *Fat Ella* on your exam). But the process of forming the link will, more often than not, obviate the problem because the link to the original item is made stronger by the act of forming these crazy associations. And, again, the crazier they are, the more *memorable* they are.

In the next chapter, we'll get away from straight factual memory for a little while and talk about how we can get a better grasp of material as we read through it the first time.

Chapter Four

READING AND REMEMBERING

Nothing you do as you pursue your studies *in any subject* will serve you as well as learning to read...and remembering what you've read, whenever you need to. The ability to recall a great amount of detail with*out* having to review is a tremendous benefit to *any* student.

In college, where the reading demands of a *single* course can be voluminous, just think how much more students could get out of texts and how much more efficiently they could prepare for exams and term papers *if* they could get most of the information they need *the first time around!*

This chapter will show you how to do it...easily.

Reading to remember

The best way to begin any reading assignment is to skim the pages to get an overall view of what information is included in the text. Then, read the entire text slowly and carefully and highlight the text and/or take notes in your notebook.

I'm going to digress for a moment, taking *your* side, to criticize a large number, perhaps even the majority, of the texts you're forced to plow through. This criticism is constructive: I want to show you the deficiencies in textbooks that you will have to overcome in order to be the best student you can be *without unnecessary effort.*

Think of the differences in writing and presentation between newspapers and textbooks. Newspapers are edited and designed to make reading simple. Most newspaper articles are organized using the "pyramid" approach: The first paragraph (the top of the pyramid) makes the major point of the story, then successive paragraphs add more detail and make related points, filling out the pyramid. So, you can get a pretty good handle on the day's news by reading the headlines and the first few paragraphs of each story. Interested in more details? Just read on.

Textbooks, on the other hand, usually are *not* written to allow for such an approach. Many times authors begin with a relatively general introduction to the material to be covered, and then lead readers through their reasoning to major points.

The next time you have to read a history, geography or similar text, try skimming the assigned pages first. Read the heads, the subheads and the call outs, those brief notes or headings in the outside margins of each page that summarize the topic covered in the paragraph or section. Read the first sentence of each paragraph. Then go back and start reading the details.

To summarize the skimming process:

1. Read and be sure you understand the title or heading. Try rephrasing it as a question for further clarification of what you will read.

2. Examine all the subheadings, illustrations and graphics—these will help you identify the significant matter within the text.

3. Read *thoroughly* the introductory paragraphs, the summary at the end and any questions at chapter's end.

4. Read the first sentence of every paragraph—this generally includes the main idea.

5. Evaluate what you have gained from this process: Can you answer the questions at the end of the chapter? Could you intelligently participate in a class discussion of the material?

6. Write a brief summary that capsulizes what you have learned from your skimming.

7. Based on this evaluation, decide whether a more thorough reading is required.

I've found that the most effective way to read a textbook is to first go through reading the headlines, subheadings and the callouts so that I know the major points of the chapter *before* I get to them. Then I'm more attuned to absorb when I arrive at these sections. In other words, by the time I get to the material for which I am reading the chapter, my antennae are up and my mind is ready to soak everything up.

One chapter at a time

Sometimes students have a desire to rush through the reading of textbooks to "get it over with." Granted, there are textbook writers who seem to go out of their way to encourage such a reaction. But don't fall into the trap.

Instead, before getting to the next chapter as rapidly as possible, stop to perform the following exercise:

- Write down in your notebook the definitions of any key terms you think are essential to *understanding* the topic.

- Write down questions and answers that you think help *clarify* the topic. Play teacher for a minute and design a "pop" quiz on the chapter.

- Write questions for which you *don't have the answers* and then go back and find them—by rereading the chapter, noting questions you would like to ask the professor, or through further reading.

When reading is a formula

Texts for mathematics, economics and science require a slightly different treatment. You should follow the steps outlined above, but with one important addition: Make sure that you thoroughly understand the concepts expressed in the various charts and graphs and do *not* move on to the next section unless you have mastered the previous one..

You must understand one section before moving on to the next, since the next concept is usually based on the previous one. If there are sample problems, solve those that tie in with the section you have just read to make sure you understand the concepts imparted. If you still fail to grasp a key concept, equation, etc., start again and try again. But *don't* move on—you'll just be wasting your time.

These texts really require such a slow, steady approach, even one with a lot of backtracking or, for that matter, a lot of wrong turns. "Trial and error" *is* an accepted method of scientific research. The key, though, is to make it *informed* trial and error—having a clear idea of where you're heading and *learning* from each error. While trial and error is okay, it is much more important to be able to easily apply the same analysis (solution, reasoning) to a slightly different problem, which requires real understanding. Getting the right answer just because you eliminated every *wrong* one may be a very viable strategy for taking a test but it's a lousy way to assure yourself you've actually learned something.

Understanding is especially essential in any technical subjects. Yes, it's easy for some of you to do great on math tests because you have a great memory and/or are lucky and/or have an innate math "sense." Trust me, sooner or later, your luck runs out, your memory overloads and your calculations become "sense"-less. You *will* reach a point where, without understanding, you will be left confused on the shore, watching your colleagues stroke heroically off to the promised land.

Whether math and science come easily to you or make you want to find the nearest pencil-pocketed computer nerd and throttle him, there are some ways you can do better at such technical subjects, without the world's greatest memory, a lot of luck or any "radar":

- Whenever you can, "translate" formulas and numbers into words. To test your understanding, try to put your translation into *different* words.

- Even if you're not particularly visual, pictures can often help. Try translating a particularly vexing math problem into a drawing or diagram.

- Before you even get down to solving a problem, is there any way for you to estimate the answer or, at least, to estimate the range within which the answer should fall (greater than 1, but less than 10)? This is the easy way to at least make sure you wind up in the right ballpark.

- Play around. There are often different paths to the same solution, or even equally valid solutions. If you find one, try to find others. This is a great way to increase your understanding of all the principles involved.

- When you are checking your calculations, try working *back*wards. I've found it an easier way to catch simple arithmetical errors.

- Try to figure out what is being asked, what principles are involved, what information is important, what's not. (I can't resist an example here, one that was thrown at me in 8th grade: A plane crashed in the mountains right on the Canadian-U.S. border. After it stopped sliding, approximately one-half of the now broken jet was in each country. The plane was 424 feet long, 38 feet wide, with a wingspan of 284 feet. It landed at a speed of 47 knots and traveled 4,290 before it came to a complete stop. The passengers consisted of 47 women, 142 men and 38 children. The flight crew was 4 men and 6 women. A careful inventory showed the plane broke into 147 various pieces, 67% of which were in the USA.

    Got it? OK, here's the question: In which country were the survivors buried?)

- Teach someone else. Trying to explain mathematical concepts to someone else will quickly pinpoint what you really know or don't know. It's virtually impossible to get someone else—especially someone who is slower than you at all this stuff—to understand if you don't!

(By the way, the answer is "You don't bury *survivors!*" In case you didn't notice, *none* of the mathematical information given had the slightest bearing on the answer.)

If there are sample problems, make sure that you solve them to ensure that you understand the concepts contained in the chapter. If you fail to grasp a key concept or equation, start again and try again. *Don't* move on. You'll be wasting your time.

You should approach foreign language texts the same way, especially basic texts that teach vocabulary (we'll deal with memorizing vocabulary words in the next chapter) and fundamental rules of grammar. If you haven't mastered the words you're supposed to in the first section, you'll have trouble reading the story at the end of the third.

Graffiti bridge

When I discovered highlighters during my first year of college, my reaction was, "Where have you been all my life"? I couldn't believe how terrific they were for zeroing in on the really important material in a text. However, I soon realized that I was highlighting *too much*—rereading highlighted sections became nearly the same as reading the whole darn text again.

So, I developed this set of rules for making the most of my highlighters when my work load became much heavier—during college:

1. I highlighted areas of the text with which I didn't feel completely comfortable.

2. I identified single words and sentences that encapsulated a section's major ideas and themes.

3. I underlined to make studying easier. I concentrated on the key words, facts and concepts, and skipped the digressions, multiple examples and unnecessary explanations.

4. I underlined my classroom notes as well as texts to make studying from *them* easier.

To sharpen your underlining skills, read through the next three paragraphs and indicate with your highlighter the key sentence(s) or words:

When told to communicate, most people immediately think of writing or speaking—verbal communication. Yet, there is another form of communication that everyone uses—without realizing it. Through various facial expressions, body movements and gestures, we all have a system of nonverbal communication.

We constantly signal to others our feelings and attitudes unconsciously through actions we may not even realize we are performing. One type is called barrier signals. Since most people usually feel safer behind a barrier, they often unthinkingly fold their arms or find some other pretext for placing their arms in front of their body when they feel insecure.

Such nonverbal communication can lead to serious misunderstanding if you are not careful. Take the simple symbol you make by forming a circle with your thumb and forefinger. In

America it means "OK." In France, however, it signifies a zero, something—or someone—worthless. Imagine the offense a French waiter might take if you signified your satisfaction with your meal with this sign! You would offend and insult when you only intended to praise.

Which of these sentences or words will you underline? I'd probably underline "nonverbal communication", "barrier signals", "insecure" (with an arrow drawn to "barrier signals" to remind me of the reason they're used)

And I would probably underline the first sentence in the second paragraph, which summarizes the point of the article.

Would you underline anything in the third paragraph? Why? It's an example—a nice one, a simple one, an understandable one—but if you understand the concept, why do you need anything else?

If you had to review the text for an exam, you would glance at the one sentence and four or five words you highlighted to get the entire gist of the three paragraphs. This will save you a tremendous amount of time.

Retention

The word "retention" is frequently mentioned alongside "reading."

Retention is the process by which we keep imprints of past experiences in our minds, the "storage depot." Subject to other actions of the mind, what is retained can be recalled when needed. Items are retained in the same order in which they are learned. So, your studying should build one fact, one idea, one concept on another.

Broad concepts can be retained much more easily than details. Master the generalities and the details will fall into place.

If you think something is important, you will retain it more easily. An attitude that says, "I *will* retain this," *will* help you remember. So, convincing yourself that what you are studying is something you *must* retain and recall *increases* your chance of adding it to your long-term memory bank.

As I mentioned in the last chapter, let yourself react to the data you are reading. Associating new information with what you already know will make it easier to recall.

Still having trouble?

If you follow these suggestions and you're still having trouble retaining what you read, try these other ideas. They are a bit more time-consuming, but undoubtedly will help you.

Take notes

Do you own the book you're reading? Do you not care about preserving it for posterity? Then use its margins for notes. Go beyond mere highlighting to assign some ranking to the facts conveyed by the text.

I used to use a little shorthand method to help me remember written materials. I'd draw vertical lines close to the text to assign a level of importance. One vertical line meant that the material should be reviewed; two indicated that the facts were very important; asterisks would signify "learn or fail" material. I'd draw in question marks for material that I wanted one of my smarter friends or the teacher to explain further. And use circles to indicate the stuff I was dead sure would show up on the next test.

Interestingly, I found that the very act of assigning relative weights of importance to the test and keeping a lookout for test material helped me remember because it heightened my attention. (For a more detailed method of taking notes, see Chapter 6.)

Become an active reader

Earlier in this chapter, I urged you to quiz yourself on written material to ascertain how well you'd retained it. If this doesn't work, try asking the questions *before* you read the material.

For instance, even though I have been an avid reader throughout much of my academic life, I had some trouble with the reading comprehension sections of standardized tests the first couple of times I attempted them. Why? I think I had a tendency to rush through these sections.

Then, someone suggested to me that I read the questions *before* I read the passage. And presto! Great scores in reading comp! (765 on my verbal SAT for you doubters.)

While you won't always have such a ready-made list of questions, there are other sources—the summaries at the beginnings of chapters, the synopses in tables of contents. Pay attention to these.

For instance, if an author states in an introductory paragraph, "Containing the Unsatisfactory Result of Oliver's Adventure; and a Conversation of Some Importance Between Harry Maylie and Rose," as Charles Dickens does in *Oliver Twist,* you may ask yourself:

- What was Oliver's unsatisfactory adventure?

- What could the result of it have been?

- What could Harry and Rose be talking about that's so important?

Believe it or not, this technique will train your mind to hone in on those important details when they arise in the story. It would also be a good idea to ask yourself these questions immediately after you finish the chapter. It will help you ascertain whether you "got" the important points of the chapter and help you retain the information longer.

Understand, don't memorize

Approach any text with the intent of *understanding* it rather than memorizing it. Understanding is a key part of memorization. Don't stop the flow of information during your reading (other than to underline and note). Go back and memorize later.

Organize the material

Our minds crave order. Optical illusions work because our mind is bent on imposing order on every piece of information coming in from the senses. As you are reading, think of ways to organize the material to help your mind absorb it.

I always liked diagrams with single words and short phrases connected with arrows to show cause and effect relationships. Or I would highlight in texts the *reasons* things occurred with a special mark (I used a triangle).

Develop good reading habits

It's impossible for anyone to remember what they've read at three in the morning, or while they were waiting to go out on the biggest date of their lives. Set aside quiet time when you're at your best.

Are you a morning person? Then wake up early to do your reading. Do you get going at 6:00 p.m.? Then, get your reading done before stopping by the Rathskeller.

Oh yeah. And don't forget to use your dictionary to look up terms you don't understand. (Or put the information in the next chapter to use. Then you won't need a dictionary!)

On we go

Each time you attempt to read something that you must recall, use this six-step process to assure that you will remember:

1. Evaluate the material and define your purpose for reading. Identify your interest level, and get a sense of how difficult the material is.

2. Choose appropriate reading techniques for the purpose of your reading. If you are reading to grasp the main idea, then that is exactly what you will recall.

3. Identify the important facts and remember what you need to. Let your purpose for reading dictate what you remember, and identify associations that connect the details to recall.

4. Take notes. Use your own words to give a synopsis of the main ideas. Use an outline, a diagram, or a concept tree to show relationship and pattern. Your notes provide an important backup to your memory. Writing down the key points will further reinforce your ability to remember.

5. Review. Quiz yourself on those things you *must* remember. Develop some system by which you review notes at least three times before you are required to recall. The first review should be shortly after you have read; the second should come a few

days later; and the final review should take place just before you are expected to recall. This process will help you avoid cram sessions.

6. Implement. Find opportunities to *use* the knowledge you have gained. Study groups and class discussions are invaluable opportunities to put what you have learned to good use. Participate in group discussions—they'll greatly increase what you recall.

If you find after all this work that you need still *more* help with reading, comprehension and recall, I recommend *Improve Your Reading,* one of the other volumes in my **HOW TO STUDY** *Program.*

Chapter Five

REMEMBERING THOSE 50 CENT WORDS

William F. Buckley, watch out.

The whole demeanor of Mr. Buckley, star moderator of *"Firing Line"*—all pursed lips and raised eyebrows—implies that becoming a master of vocabulary is more difficult than it really is. (Unless of course, you attend or graduated from Yale, in which case it may well *be* difficult—at least that's one Princetonian's erudite opinion.)

No, the way to a great vocabulary is at your fingertips (and it has zip to do with those Word-A-Day calendars).

In this chapter, I will show you two ways to improve your memory for sesquipedalian (having many syllables) and small, obscure words.

The building blocks method

Whenever possible, try to remember *concepts* rather than memorizing random data. For instance, if someone told you to memorize a long string of numbers—e.g., 147101316192225—it would be far better to note that each number is three higher than the one before and simply remember that rule.

Similarly, it is far better to absorb the way *words* are constructed, to memorize a relatively small number of prefixes, suffixes and roots, rather than trying to cram *Webster's Dictionary* into your already crowded memory.

A note on English

Our borrowed mother tongue, English, is perhaps the most democratic of all languages. Built on a Celtic base, it has freely admitted a multitude of words from other languages, particularly French, Latin, Greek, German, and a rich body of slang (from anywhere we could get it).

The oldest of these branches in a diverse family tree, Celtic and Old English are the least amenable to some of the techniques we are about to learn. These are basically simple words, not built in complicated fashion as are Latinate and Greek verbiages.

However, as any crossword puzzle addict can tell you, our language is replete with myriad Romance words (those from French, Italian and Spanish) that often can be dissected into rather simple elements.

The roots of language

Here are 22 roots from Latin and Greek that contribute to thousands of English words:

Root	Meaning	Example
annu	year	annual
aqua	water	aquarium
bio	life	biology
cap, capt	take, seize	capture

dic, dict	say	indicate
duc, duct	lead	induction
fact, fect	do, make	effective
fer	carry, bear	infer
graph	write	graphics
logos	word	logical
manu	hand	manufacture
mitt,miss	send	remittance
path	feel, feeling	apathy
plico	fold	implication
pon, posit	place, put	imposition
port	carry	export
psyche	mind	psychopathic
tend, tent	stretch	intention
tene,tent	have, hold	tenacious
spec	observe, see	speculative
vert	turn	introverted

The cart before the horse

As the examples above suggest, a root alone is usually not enough. Prefixes, fragments added to the beginning of a word, can greatly change the message conveyed by the root. Here are some examples of common prefixes:

Prefix	**Meaning**	**Example**
a, ab	from, away	aberration
a, an	without, not	amoral
ad, af, at, ag	to, toward	admonition, affection, aggressor
ambi	both	ambiguous
amphi	around	amphitheater
ant, anti	against	antidote
ante	before	antecedent
cata	down, under	catacomb

con, com	with, together	commitment
contra	against	contraband
de	away from	deviant
di	separate	divorce
dia	through	diameter
dis	apart, opposite	disrespect
e, ex	out of, over	exorbitant
em	out	embalm
en	in	envelope
hyper	above, over	hyperthermia
hypo	under	hypoglycemic
il, im, in	not	illicit, impeccable, incomprehensive
inter	between	intercept, interloper
intra	within	intramural, intraparty
ir	not	irreligious
per	through	perspicacious
peri	around	peripheral
post	after	postmortem
pre	before	premonition
pro	for, forth	production
re	again, back	regression
sub, sup	under	substantiate
super	over, above	supercede, supernatural
trans	across	transportation, transmission
un	not	uncool

The tail that wags the dog

And the last, but certainly not the least important building block of words is the suffix, which quite often indicates how the word is being used. Suffixes can be used to turn an adjective into an adverb (the "ly" ending), to compare things (smallER, smallEST), or even added onto other suffixes (liveLIEST). Some suffixes with which you should be familiar are:

Suffix	Meaning	Example
-able, -ible	capable of	pliable
-ac, -al, -ial	pertaining to	hypochondriac;remedial
-acy	quality of	fallacy; legacy
-ance, -ence	state of being	abundance
-ant, -ent	one who...	student
-dom	quality of	martyrdom
-er, -or	one who...	perpetrator
-ion	act of	extermination
-ish, ity	quality of	purplish, enmity
-ive	state of being	active, decisive
-less	lacking	penniless
-ly	like	fatherly, scholarly
-ment	process of	enlightenment
-ness	state of	holiness, cleanliness
-ose	full of	grandiose, verbose
-ry	state of	ribaldry, mimicry

Practice those —fixes

Of course, I don't expect that you'll memorize these lists. But if you read them over a few times, paying particular attention to the examples, you'll absorb the roots, prefixes and suffixes fairly quickly.

Here's a list of 50 words. Write the definition in the blank space using what you remember of the building blocks of words above. Then, check to see how you did using the lists above.

Peripheral_____

Supercilious_____

Apocryphal_____

Perspicacious _____

Psychographic _____

Improve Your Memory

Aqueous_____

Introspective _____

Subjudice _____

Contentious _____

Transponder _____

Atrophy_____

Complected _____

Emulate_____

Avocation_____

Contravene _____

Presentiment _____

Ductile _____

Neologism _____

Implicit _____

Austerity_____

Intemperate_____

Replicate _____

Prodigal_____

Admonition_____

Subtend _____

Punctulate_____

Intermittent _____

Versatile_____

Rudimentary_____

Transubstantiate _____

Conurbation _____

Annuity_____

Hyperthermia _____

Preposterous_____

Imbroglio_____

Hypertense_____

Antipathy _____

Regression_____

Psychedelic_____

Aberration_____

Detraction_____

Interpolate_____

Hypoallergenic_____

Intangible_____

Antiestablishmentarianism_____

Parochialism_____

Overcontentious_____

Retreatant_____

Discrepant_____

Induction_____

Method with madness in it

How did you do on the quiz? I'll bet a lot better than you thought, simply because of this rather brief introduction to etymology.

But now, let's examine another way of remembering words so that you can have powerful words at your disposal—the soundalike method. As we saw in Chapter 3, forming associations—sometimes rather outrageous ones—can be quite helpful in carving easy-access roads to the long-term memory banks.

To use this method, create a scenario using the soundalike of the word or parts of the word and the definition of the word.

Consider this example: Let's say that you've seen the word "ostracize" countless times, but can never quite remember that it means "to cast out from society." You could then create this nonsense thought: "The ostrich's eyes are so big, no one wants to look at him."

In such an example, you would be using the size of the ostrich and creating an absurd reason he might be a cast out. Or, I could have made the phrase: "The ostrich's size was so big he was thrown out of his hole."

Oh sure, you're saying, that's an easy example. But let's take another one. Since we're in a chapter on vocabulary, let's consider "sesquipedalian," which means "having many syllables" or "tending to use long words." Our soundalike association could be: "She says quit pedaling those big words."

Or, one picture might be worthy of a particular vocabulary word. You might associate the difficult-to-remember word not with a phrase, but with an outrageous picture.

For instance, to remember that the word "flambe" means a food covered with flames, think of a plate of food with bees whose wings are ablaze flying from it.

Again, as we learned in Chapter 3, this sort of exercise is not a lot of work, but it can be a great deal of fun. And it will help your mind hold onto words—even those you use infrequently—forever.

Here's a list of "50 cent words" with soundalikes that will make them easy to learn:

Allay (to calm or put at rest):
"I'll lay me down to sleep."

Bachanalia (a drunken party):
"There's a great party back in the alley."

Braggadocio (empty boasting or bragging)
Picture a man with the word "brag" on his hat at a square dance... "do-ci-do"ing!

Churlish (ill-mannered or rude):
"My curl is one that just won't behave."

Depilatory (substance that removes unneccessary hair):
Picture yourself shaving a pill in a laboratory.

Espouse (to give support to a cause):
"A spouse usually will support you." Or picture a bride or groom holding you up.

Extemporize (to speak or perform without prior preparation)
"That dog on the podium has distempered eyes"

Feral (wild, untamed):
"The bar fight was a free fer all."

Gregarious (enjoying others' company):
"Gregory is a friendly guy."

Howdah (a seat for two on an elephant's back)
Picture yourself riding on an elephant, saying "Howdah, pardner."

Inure (to accustom to something unpleasant):
"I'll stick this in your face until you get used to it."

Jejune (inadequate, not nourishing):
"Hey, June, I'm starved."

Kiosk (small structure in a public place for selling small articles):
Need a key? Ask that man in the booth.

Loggia (open-sided galley or arcade):
"Actor Robert Loggia went to the arcade."

Menhir (a large stone stood up in prehistoric times):
"There must have been some strong men here to lift that rock long ago."

Noisome (harmful, noxious):
A noise, some say, is very harmful.

Ostensible (pretended; professed):
"It was almost sensible to pretend."

Petard (a small bombshell):
Picture yourself walking a small bomb, painted like a playing card, on a leash.

Preponderate (To exceed something else in weight)
"The pirate's plunder weighed a lot"

Quietus (death):
"Nothing's as quiet as a cemetery."

Rueful (showing good-humored regret):
"The band Roomful of Blues was smiling."

Sanguine (hopeful, optimistic):
"I sang when I thought it would happen."

Steatopygia (extreme accumulation of fat around the buttocks)
"The cannibals found the steamed pygmy a little fatty"

Tenuous (very thin; having little substance or validity):
Picture a car with a license plate reading, "10 U US" suddenly vaporizing.

Umbrage (a feeling of being offended):
"Paying $4 to use some bridge made me angry."

Vortex (a whirling mass of water or air):
Picture four Texans being picked up by a cyclone.

Wanton (irresponsible, lacking proper restraint)
"The driver of that one-ton truck crashed into everything."

Eschew obfuscation

With this tool, you can become a horribly pedantic conversationalist and never have to run to the dictionary while you're reading *Finnegan's Wake*.

I'll bet that the simple process of reading this chapter has helped you remember the two dozen or so words above. Don't believe me?

Read through them a couple of times and try the little test that follows. Simply fill in the definition beside each word:

1. Ostracize _____

2. Sesquepedalian _____

3. Churlish _____

4. Tenuous _____

5. Petard _____

6. Quietus _____

7. Vortex _____

8. Sanguine _____

9. Rueful _____

10. Menhir _____

11. Steatopygia _____

12. Preponderate _____

How did you do? I'm sure you're on the road to a better vocabulary. So, keep up the good work. In a short while, the task of coming up with soundalikes, associations and outrageous mental images will be second nature to you.

Try a sample

Still another method that works quite well—and is relatively easy to employ for some words—is to associate a word with a very particular example. If you're reading an English grammar textbook and you come across the term "oxymoron," which is defined as "a figure of speech combining seemingly contradictory words or phrases," think how much easier it would be to remember if your notes looked like this:

Oxymoron	jumbo shrimp, cruel kindness
Onomatopoeia	PLOP, PLOP, FIZZ, FIZZ
Metaphor	food for thought
Simile	this is <u>like</u> that

Chapter Six

TAKING NOTES TO REMEMBER TEXTS

I have a confession to make, a rather difficult one for someone whose specialty is careers and education: To this very day, I resent having to write an outline for a book, article, or research project. I'd much rather just sit down and start writing.

I would have hated myself in school if I knew then what I know now: You should do outlines while you are *reading,* as well. The fact is, outlines will help you review a text more quickly and remember it more clearly.

In Chapter 4, we advised using highlighters to, well, highlight important messages. This is great in a relatively easy-to-remember text. For other courses, it would be a sure sign of masochism, as it assures only one thing: you will have to read a great deal of your deadly textbooks all over again when exam time rolls around.

Likewise, marginalia usually make the most sense only in context, so the messy method of writing small notes in all white space around the text will engender a great deal of rereading as well.

So then, what's *the* most effective way to read and remember your textbooks? *Sigh.* Yes, that good, old outline.

Reverse engineering

Outlining a textbook, article or other secondary source is a little bit like Japanese "reverse engineering"—a way of developing a schematic for something so that you can see exactly how it's been put together. Seeing that logic of construction will help you a great deal in remembering the book—by putting the author's points down in *your* words, you will be building a way to retrieve the key points of the book more easily from your memory.

What's more, outlining will force you to distinguish the most important points from those of secondary importance, helping you build a true understanding of the topic.

The bare bones of outlining

Standard outlines use Roman numerals, (I, II, III, etc.), capital letters, Arabic numerals (1, 2, 3, 4...), and lower-case letters and indentations to show the relationships between and importance of topics in the text. While you certainly don't have to use the Roman-numeral system, your outline would be organized in the following manner:

Title
Author
I. First important topic in the text
    A. First subtopic
        1. First subtopic of A

    a. First subtopic of 1

    b. Second subtopic of 1

  2. Second subtopic of A

II. The second important topic in the text

Get the idea? In a book, the Roman numerals usually would refer to chapters; the capital letters to subheadings; and the Arabic numbers and lower-case letters to blocks of paragraphs. In an article or single chapter, the Roman numbers would correspond to subheadings, capital letters to blocks of paragraphs, Arabic numerals to paragraphs, small letters to key sentences.

What's he getting at?

We understand things in outline form. Ask an intelligent person to recount something and he'll state the main points and only enough details to make his words interesting and understandable. The discipline of creating outlines will help you zero in on the most important points an author is making and capture them, process them, and, thereby, retain them.

Sometimes an author will have the major point of a paragraph in the first sentence. But just as often, the main idea of a paragraph or section will follow some of these telltale words: therefore, because, thus, since, as a result.

When you see any of these words, you should identify the material they introduce as the major points in your outline. Material immediately preceding and following almost always will be in support of these major points.

Create a time line

I always found it frustrating to read textbooks in social studies. I'd go through chapters on France, England, the Far

East, and have a fairly good understanding of those areas, but have no idea where certain events stood in a global context. As more and more colleges add multicultural curricula, you may find it even more difficult to "connect" events in 17th-century France or 19th-century Africa with what was happening in the rest of the world (let alone the U.S.).

An excellent tool for overcoming that difficulty is a time line that you can update periodically. It will help you visualize the chronology and remember the relationship of key world events.

For instance, a time line for the earliest years in the history of the United States might look like this (I would suggest a horizontal time line, but the layout of this book makes reproducing it that way difficult. So here's a vertical version):

1776———The American Revolution
1783———The Articles of Confederation
1786———Shay's Rebellion
1789———Ratification of the Constitution
1791———The Federal Reserve Bank
1795———The XYZ Affair
1798———The Alien and Sedition Laws

Comparing this to other time lines in your notebook would put these events in the context of the end of the Napoleonic Era and the French Revolution.

Draw a concept tree

Another terrific device for limiting the amount of verbiage in your notes and making them more memorable is the concept tree. Like a time line, the concept tree is a visual representation of the relationship among several key facts. For instance, one might depict the system of government in the United States this way:

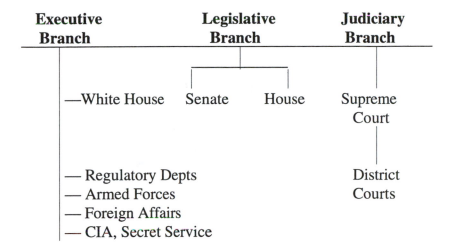

Such devices certainly give further credence to the old saying, "A picture is worth a thousand words," since time lines and concept trees will be much more helpful than mere words in remembering material, particularly conceptual material. And developing them will ensure that your interest in the text will not flag too much.

Add a vocabulary list

Many questions on exams require students to define the terminology in a discipline. Your physics professor will want to know what "vectors" are, while your calculus teacher will want to know about "differential equations." Your history professor will want you to be well-versed on "The Cold War," and your English Lit professor will require you to know about the "Romantic Poets."

Therefore, as I read my textbooks, I was sure to write down all new terms and definitions in my notes and draw a little box around them, because I knew these were among the most likely items to be asked about on tests and that the box would always draw my attention to them when I was reviewing.

Most textbooks will provide definitions of key terms. However, if your textbook does *not* define a key term, make sure you write the term down in your notes *with* a definition. And remember that your notes should reflect *your* understanding of the term. Take the time to rephrase and write it in your own words. This will help you remember it.

Wait, you're not done yet!

After you've finished making notes on a chapter, go through them and identify the most important points—the ones that might turn up on tests—either with an asterisk or by highlighting them. You'll probably end up marking about 40 or 50 percent of your entries.

When you're reviewing for a test, you should read all the notes, but your asterisks will indicate which points you considered the most important *while the chapter was fresh in your mind*.

To summarize, when it comes to taking notes from your texts or other reading material, you should:

- Take a cursory look through the chapter *before* you begin reading. Look for subheads, highlighted terms and summaries at the end of the chapter to give you a sense of the content.

- Read each section thoroughly. While your review of the chapter "clues" will help your understanding of the material, you should read for comprehension rather than speed.

- Make notes immediately after you've finished reading, using the outline, time line and concept tree and vocabulary list methods of organizations as necessary.

- Mark with an asterisk or highlight the key points as you review your notes.

Chapter Seven

REMBRING HOW TOO SPEL GUD

Every time I have my daughter read to me, I become aware of the difficulties of spelling in English. What's that "k" doing on the edge of the knife, and why didn't someone put the lights out on that "gh" in night? How come graffiti has two "f"'s and one "t" while spaghetti doubles the "t" (and pronounces the "gh" as a hard "g"!)?

Well, one way to win the spelling bee in your town is to have a great vocabulary, using some of the suggestions mentioned in Chapter 5. Another way is to learn the rules of English spelling, then make special note of the rather frequent exceptions to those rules.

Double or nothing

Many people make mistakes on words with doubled consonants. The most common quick-repeating consonants are "l", "n", "p", and "s", but "t" and "r" repeat fairly often, too.

While the incidence of these doubles might seem accidental or arbitrary, they usually follow these rules:

Double "*l*": Usually result from adding suffixes ending in "l" to roots beginning with the letter, vice versa for suffixes. Examples: alliterative, unusually. However, alien does *not* have a double "l" because it is itself a root.

Double "*n*": A similar rule applies to "n"s. Double "n"s usually result from adding a suffix that turns an adjective ending in "n" into a noun (wantonness or thinness) or "-ny", which turns a noun ending in "n" into an adjective (funny).

Double "*p*"s "*r*"s and "*s*"s don't generally have a hard-and-fast rule, so you'll usually have to rely on other tricks of memory. For instance, I've always had trouble spelling "embarrassment" (double "r" *and* double "s") since it certainly doesn't seem to follow the same rule as "harassment" (double "s" only).

In these cases, you'll have to associate some rule with the word. When I worked as a reporter, you'd often hear people answer questions about spelling in such codes. "Four 's's and two 'p's" is the answer to "How do you spell Mississippi?" I remember the rule for "harassment" by imagining someone pushing away (or harassing) the "r" some part of my brain insists should be there.

Double "*r*"s and double "*t*"s and other doubles occurring (note the double "r"!) before -ed:

1. If the word ends in a single consonant (occuR, omiT)
2. If the word is accented on the last syllable (comPEL, reMIT)

Is it "i" before "e" or...?

The general rule is: "I" before "e" except after "c" or when it sounds like "a", as in "neighbor" and "weigh." This rule holds, with some exceptions: seize, leisure, caffeine and the names of other chemical compounds.

Honest able

Many people get thrown over words ending in "e" that have -able or -ible added to them. What to do with that final "e"? Well, here are some rules:

- *Keep the final "e"* for words ending in -ice, -ace or -ge. Someone is embracEABLE and situations are managEABLE.
- *Drop that final "e"* when it is preceded by any consonant other than "c" or "g" (unlovable).

Other rules for adding suffixes to words ending in "e":

- Retain the "e" when adding "-ly" and "-ment" (unless the word ends in "-dge". It's judgment, *not* judgEment).
- Drop the "e" before adding "y" as a suffix (phony).
- Drop the final "e" and add "-ible" to words ending in "-nce", "-uce" or "-rce" (producible, unconvincible).
- Use "-ible" for words ending in "-miss" (dismissible).

Rules are meant to be broken

The English language is based on Celtic, Norwegian, German, Latin, French and several other languages. As a result, it veers from the rules fairly often. So, while these guidelines certainly will help you a great deal, sometimes you will have to rely on association and some of the other methods we spoke of in other chapters to remember all the *exceptions* to them.

Chapter Eight

HOW TO REMEMBER *ANY* NUMBER

Up until now, we've been dealing in the rich world of words. Anything having to do with words is a relatively easy task for the memory because words always can be associated with *things*, which, because they can be seen, touched, heard and smelled, can carry more than one association and, therefore, be easier to remember.

But a number is an abstraction. Unless associated with something, it is relatively difficult to remember. For instance, most people have tremendous difficulty remembering telephone numbers that they've only heard once. The reason is that a phone number doesn't usually conjure up an image or a sensation. It is merely 7 or 10 digits without a relationship to one another or to you.

You can change that

The trick, then, is to establish more associations for numbers.

But how? After all, they can be so abstract. It would be like trying to remember colors without having the benefit of *things* associated with those colors.

In early grade school (first, to be exact) I learned one of the first associations that helped me remember the order of colors in the spectrum: **ROY G. BIV**, which stands for: **R**ed, **O**range, **Y**ellow, **G**reen, **B**lue, **I**ndigo, **V**iolet.

Well, the idea with numbers is to create words from them that are similarly memorable.

Making friends with numbers

Numbers are infinite, but the system we use to designate them is even more user-friendly than the alphabet. It consists of 10 digits that all of you should know by now (just follow the bouncing ball): 0, 1, 2, 3, 4, 5, 6, 7, 8, and 9.

The trick to the mnemonic alphabet—a rather popular technique for remembering numbers—is turning those numbers into the equivalent of letters, symbols that represent sounds. The pioneer of this concept is Harry Lorayne, author of many books on memory. His method calls for associating the 10 familiar Arabic numerals with a sound or a related group of sounds.

Here's how this brilliantly simple scheme works:

> 1 = T, D
> 2 = N
> 3 = M
> 4 = R
> 5 = L
> 6 = J, soft G, CH, SH, DG, TCH
> 7 = K, hard C, hard G, Q
> 8 = F, V, PH
> 9 = P, B
> 0 = Z, soft C, S

You're probably thinking, "What sense does this all make, and how in heck am I supposed to remember it?"

Well, though this seems like madness, believe me, there's some extraordinarily wonderful method in it.

The number "1" is a single keystroke, as is the letter "T". "D" is a suitable substitute because it is pronounced almost the same way as "T"—by touching the tongue to the front of the roof of the mouth.

Two is represented by "N" because "N" has *two* downstrokes.

"M" is a stand-in for "3" because, you guessed it, it has *three* downstrokes.

Four is represented by "R" because the dominant sound in the word "four" is the -RRRRRR at the end.

The Romans used "L" to represent 50. Also if you fan out the fingers of your left hand as if to say, "It's 5 o'clock," your index finger and thumb form the letter "L".

Hold a mirror up to a "6" and you get a "J", particularly if you write as badly as I do. Therefore, all letters pronounced like "J"—by touching your tongue to the inside of your lower teeth—are acceptable substitutes for "6".

Place two "7"'s back to back, turning one upside down, and what do you have? Right, a "K". All of those letter sounds formed in the back of the mouth, as is "K", are therefore potential substitutes for the lucky "7".

Draw a line parallel to the ground through a handwritten "8" and you'll have a creature that resembles a script, lower case "F". Therefore, all sounds formed by placing the top teeth on the lower lip can represent "8".

Once again, I invoke my mirror, mirror on the wall to show that a "9" and a capital "P" are virtually identical. "B", also formed by putting your lips together, is a substitute for "9" anytime.

And "0" is an easy one. Zero begins with a "Z", so any sound formed by hissing through the space between flat tongue and roof of mouth is acceptable.

Now what?

Believe me, this device, which probably seems very ungainly to you now, is a terrific way to remember numbers. Go over the list above a few more times, cover it up, and take the little quiz below, matching numbers with appropriate sounds and vice-versa.

8 _____

K _____

Z _____

2 _____

T _____

Q _____

4 _____

S _____

L _____

3 _____

Consonantal divide

Have you noticed that all of the sounds used in the mnemonic alphabet are consonants? That's because users of the system should be free to use vowels however they please around these consonants to form words or memorable sounds.

Therefore the number "15" can be "QueeN". Or the number of that wonderful person you met in the Rathskeller today and would so like to see again could be "vasectomy to go", or 806-1316 (VSCTMTG).

How about trying to remember pi to 7 places. You could try to memorize 3.141592 or just think, "MeTRic TalL PeNny" or "My TReaT LoPed iN."

A great date

One of the most useful applications of this method is remembering dates and tying them to events. If you wanted to remember, for example, "William the Conqueror invaded England in 1066," you could endlessly repeat that sentence, or you could remember, "Bill THiS eGG." Combining these methods with the chain-link technique we discussed in earlier chapters, you could imagine an egg rolling off the white cliffs of Dover, where William first landed. (Alternately, you can make up a ridiculous but simple rhyme like, "In 1066, Billy C ate fish and chips" that would also work just fine.)

Now you try it. Make up phrases using the mnemonic alphabet equivalents for your Social Security number, the first three phone numbers in your little black book, or the times for high and low tide tomorrow. Then try the below quiz, writing in first the letter equivalents for the numbers, then a brief word, phrase or sentence that would help you remember it. I've done the first one for you.

947568	PRKLGF	PeRry KiLled the GolFball
		(or PoRK LoG loaF)
844941	_____	_____

671024	_____	_____
95776002	_____	_____
84712457	_____	_____
746603201	_____	_____
1234567890	_____	_____
0967854213	_____	_____

What about even longer numbers? How do you remember 20, 30, even 50-digit numbers without trying to hard? Well, you could make your "story sentences" longer. But you can also group the numbers into a series of pictures. For example, let's say you had to remember the number "289477500938177101550"—21 digits! Try grouping it into smaller number combinations, creating a picture for each. In this case, I've managed with only two pictures:

289477 can be represented by NVPRGK or a picture of a sailor (NaVy) PouRing GunK.

500938 is LZZBMV. *How* is the sailor standing? LaZily. Where is he standing? Right By a MoVie theatre. (See it in your head.)

177101550. What's playing? DeBBie DoeS DaLLaS. (Now you know why he wasn't paying attention to the gunk!)

Can you see how you could easily memorize a 50-digit number with just four or five pictures? Try it yourself. You'll see how easy it is.

Everybody loves them dead presidents

Or so sang bluesman Willie Dixon, referring to the presidential portraits that grace our folding money. But he could just as easily have been referring to your least favorite history professor—you know, the one who expects you to know who was the 23rd president of the United States? (By the way, that was Harrison, and the way we will remember that is "No ('n' represents 2), My ('m' is for 3) hairy son."

Now you try it. Here are the dozen most recent U.S. presidents. How are you going to remember them?

30. Coolidge
31. Hoover
32. Roosevelt
33. Truman
34. Eisenhower
35. Kennedy
36. Johnson
37. Nixon
38. Ford
39. Carter
40. Reagan
41. Bush
42. Clinton

How did you do?

Here's how I would use mnemonics to establish a chain link between some of the names and numbers:

Coolidge: "The MouSe (30) gave the knife a cool edge."
Hoover: Picture a MaD (31) vacuum cleaner.

Roosevelt: "MoNey (32) belt Roosevelt"

Truman: "If it's not true, man, stay MuM (33)".

Eisenhower: Picture Ike behind a lawn MoweR (34)

Get the idea? This is an absolutely invaluable tool. It will empower you to remember phone numbers in the Rathskeller without resorting to writing on wet cocktail napkins. Perhaps more important, it will help you remember dates and facts without incessantly repeating them.

Chapter Nine

REMEMBERING NAMES AND FACES

Like it or not, you're not going to be in school for the rest of your life. Soon, you will begin to look for a job, to string together a "network" of acquaintances and contacts that will help lift you onto that first rung of the corporate ladder.

You'll participate in that horrible convention called the "cocktail party" and other social events where you'll be expected to be charming.

Every once in a while, I go to a cocktail party, if only to remind myself why I don't do it more often. But seriously, cocktail parties give me a chance to practice a skill that I consider one of the key reasons for my earlier success as an advertising salesperson: remembering the names (and some of the other pertinent personal data) that went with the faces.

In fact, one of the principle reasons I became interested in the subject of memory improvement was that I was tired of calling people "pal" and "buddy" when I could *not* remember their names after they said to *me,* "Hey, Ron, how have you been?"

You can avoid those embarrassing moments forever by memorizing these key steps to link a person's face and name in your memory forever.

Take a good look

Whenever you meet someone, look him or her in the face and make special note of some outstanding feature. Does the person have a big nose? Huge earlobes? Dimples? Big, beautiful blue eyes? A cleft in the chin? A mole? It doesn't have to be a particularly ugly or beautiful feature—just something that sets the person apart from the rest of the people in the room.

Once you've locked in on a feature, do *not* stare at it, but *do* get your imagination working—make that feature truly outstanding by embellishing it. If it's a big nose, make it as big as a toucan's beak in your mind's eye. Dimples should be as large as craters; big earlobes should dangle on the person's shoulders.

Make sure you got it

Remember my friend Tony from the Preface, the fellow who couldn't remember that his reading glasses were on top of his head?

Well, he had a similar problem with names. I remember once introducing him to three people who, along with him, were the first to arrive at my house for a little dinner party. One minute later, I went into the kitchen to fix drinks for everybody and Tony was right at my heels. "What was the name of that brunette in the miniskirt?" he asked in a hushed voice. "Monique," I said. "How 'bout the bald guy?" asked Tony. "That's Joe." Finally, very embarrassed, Tony asked, "And what about the other woman?"

There are fleas with longer memories. But now Tony prides himself on being able to remember the names of 30 or 40 people in a room after being introduced only once.

The first thing he taught himself to do was to repeat the person's name, looking right at the person as he did so. Tony, being a very charming guy, doesn't do this as if he's trying out for a lead role remake of "Being There." He repeats the name back as part of a greeting—"Nice to meet you, Monique." "Hi Joe, I've heard a lot about you. You're Ron's partner, right?"

Using such a technique, you will not only be noting the person's name, you will be making sure that you got it right.

Think of a link

Once you've done that, it's time to come up with some sort of link between the name and the feature that you've already exaggerated out of proportion.

I saw the most obvious example of this as a kid when a memorist appeared on a Sunday morning TV show. He was introduced to the 100 or so youngsters in the audience and repeated all of their names back to them at the end of the show. Asked how he had done it, he used the example of a boy named Tommy Fox. The boy had a dimple, said the memorist, so he imagined a bare meadow with a hole in the middle. A fox bounded through the hedge followed by hunters shouting, "Tommy Ho!"

Bingo! The name and the face were linked forever.

Too easy, you say?

Well, that one *is* an easy one, but it illustrates the technique quite well. Certain names do suggest pictures—Miller, Fry, Wright (a playWRIGHT or wheelWRIGHT), Silverman, Burns, Elman (a man shaped like an 'L,' of course).

Others will require the use of soundalikes—Wallace (Wallets), Depiero (The Cheerio), Gruenig (Grooming), O'Donnell (Old McDonald).

Once you've come up with these soundalikes or pictures, find some way to link them with the image you've formed of the person's chief facial features.

For instance, once I was introduced to a man named Vince Dolce (pronounced Dole-see). As I was walking toward him, I noticed some rather dark circles under his eyes. In my imagination, because I'm so accustomed to using the technique outlined above, the circles became bigger than a raccoon's. When I heard that his name was Dolce, I immediately thought, "dull sheep" and pictured tired, sleepy sheep grazing on those now even bigger circles below Vince's eyes. The sheep, of course, were bothering him, and this made him *wince* (for Vince).

That's all there is to turning a room full of strangers into people that—for better or worse—you'll never forget!

Chapter Ten

REMEMBERING A SPEECH OR ORAL REPORT

The English poet John Donne wrote, "Death be not proud," and no wonder: In many public opinion polls in which respondents were asked to rate their biggest fears, public speaking—and not the grim reaper—won...hands down.

The reasons for this are legion, but undoubtedly heading the list is the horrible idea that in mid-sentence we will go blank, completely unable to recall the brilliant speeches we'd stayed up late writing the night before.

We'll return to our seat in a muddled silence. Feeling like a naked man in a spotlight.

To make sure that doesn't happen to you, I'll teach you how to use chain links, association and all of the other tricks we've discussed in this book to help you remember speeches or oral class presentations.

Take note

Remember the outline method we spoke about in Chapter 6? Well, the way to go about preparing a speech is to outline it, write it, *re*outline it, and then use the outline as your key to remembering it. Why should you bother when you went through the trouble of writing the speech in the first place?

Well, because there are two kinds of speakers: good and dull. The good ones *talk* to you. The bad ones *read* to you. In order to be a *speaker*, rather than a *reader*, you should know your speech by heart.

A tasty toastmaster

Let's step aside from the memory issue and talk about how you should organize your speech (after all, it will be the key to remembering it well).

I've done so much public speaking throughout my career that I've actually grown to enjoy it—in fact, I look *forward* to talking to a room full of strangers. I don't think that would be the case at all were it not for a piece of valuable advice I acquired quite a few years ago. There is only one best way to organize a speech: Tell them what you are going to say; say it; then, tell them what you said.

Let's say you were assigned to take one side of an argument in a debate and your topic is, "The solution to the drug problem: Legalize all drugs." Your outline might look like this:

The Opening

I. Drugs should be legalized
II. This will help solve, not deepen, the drug crisis in the country
III. Keeping drugs illegal assures that criminals get rich and government funds go to waste

<u>The Middle</u>

I.   The reasons to legalize drugs
   A. Keeping them illegal artificially raises prices
      1. Costs are inflated 2,500 percent
   B. Public funds are being wasted
      1. Law enforcement efforts are not working
      2. Funds for rehabilitation are paltry
II. Control would be easier
   A. It has worked in other countries
   B. Licensing would increase state revenues
   C. Harsh penalties would inhibit sales to minors
   D. Drug addicts available for outreach programs
III. Prohibition doesn't work
   A. Parallels with Roaring Twenties

<u>The Closing</u>

I.   The costly, ineffective War on Drugs
II. Legalization sounds radical, but it would work
III. The alternative is far more dangerous

Commit it to memory

Once you have the outline, use the chain link method to remember the flow of your speech.

Here's how it might work for the outline above:

First, you'd remember your opening by picturing yourself at some sort of an opening—a doorway, or perhaps opening night of a play entitled, "Drug Free America." You imagine yourself walking inside the theater and seeing three scenes set from left to right:

I.   Congress enacting a law;
II. People emerging from hospital beds and saying they don't need drugs anymore;

III. Criminal types having piles of money taken from them by police.

Next, you imagine yourself sitting in the *middle* section of the theater.

I. You look at your *Playbill* and it reads:
    A. "2,500%"
    B. On the stage you see:
       1. Police in handcuffs
       2. A nurse in a clinic begging for money
       3. A schoolroom with no teacher

II. Imagine some sort of Control to remember this part of your exposition section, perhaps your foot on a gas pedal:
    A. Your foot is on the gas pedal because you're driving past an Amsterdam street or a windmill (since Holland has a model program of legalization and control);
    B. You reach for your driver's license, which has a big dollar sign on it;
    C. Out the window you see a seedy character being dragged from a schoolyard by the police;
    D. And you see that nurse in the clinic helping someone.

Then, all of a sudden, you car is cut off by gangsters being chased by police as if in a classic car chase from "The Untouchables."

Then, imagine yourself closing your car door and hearing:

I. The sounds of war. You look up and you see huge dollar signs suspended on parachutes coming down from the sky.

II. You see Karl Marx (or another "radical") in an army outfit and then,

III. A mushroom cloud or some other apocalyptic image.

Once you've conjured up a set of hooks like this, read through your speech several times, mentally flipping through the appropriate images as you do so. In that way your words and ideas will become *linked* to pictures, making them so much easier to remember.

Now you try it

Here's an oral presentation you might have to give in an Economics or Political Science class. See how you do with establishing chain links so that you can stand up and be brilliant.

Democrats Vs. Republicans
The Real Economy

The cornerstone of Republican economics is that the entire population benefits when the rich are permitted to retain more of their income for themselves. Former President Ronald Reagan believed the benefits enjoyed by wealthy Americans as a result of the 1981 tax cut would "trickle down" to all other citizens. Similarly, President Bush has advocated lowering the tax on capital gains. This would benefit the wealthy, who own most of the nation's assets, and, he contends, give a boost to the economy that would help everyone else, too.

The Democrats, on the other hand, contend that such a distribution of the tax burden is unfair. They think the federal government should increase taxes for wealthy citizens and that government should spread the wealth directly through a variety of social programs. The two sides were in a classic standoff through the 1980s. The Republicans were successful in keeping taxes on the wealthy low, while the Democrats did their best to ensure that spending on social programs stayed high. Since members from both camps thought it wise to increase military expenditures during the decade, the federal budget had nowhere to go but up.

In the budget agreement struck between Democrats and Republicans in 1990, both sides gave in a little. Taxes on the rich would increase a bit, and social ("entitlement") programs would grow when the government had the money to pay the bills.

But at the heart of this compromise, which is more like a cease-fire than a treaty to end the long war, legislators face the same choices: growth or fairness, private investment or public spending, tax cuts for the wealthy or entitlement programs for the middle class and poor. In this war, the Republicans wave the flag of pure American capitalism, with its ideals of individualism and self-determination. The Democrats, some would argue, represent the kinder, gentler side of human nature.

But is this the real choice facing America?

Many would argue that it is not. And the reason is that both sides are dead wrong. The American capitalism so dear to the Republicans is no longer dependent on the private investments of motivated, aggressive American capitalists. Future economic success in the U.S. depends instead on the country's unique qualities: the skills and insights of the work force and their application to the realities of the global economy.

The Democrats are equally wrong: The role of government is not merely to spread the wealth. It is to build "human capital" and our infrastructure. More than ever, brain power, linked by roads, airports, computers, and cables, is the key factor in determining a nation's standard of living.

OK, take a few minutes to think of the links that will help you remember this speech.

How did you do? If you didn't start by outlining this little speech, probably not so well. Here's my outline:

I.   Republicans want lower taxes for rich
    A. Benefits for all
    B. Reagan '81 tax cut
    C. Bush wants lower cap. gains tax.
II.   Democrats want higher taxes on rich
    A. More social spending; spreading the wealth
III.   The standoff.
    A. Taxes on rich low; social spending, high.
    B. Huge federal budget
IV.   Both sides wrong
    A. Reps. wrong: cap not depend prvte investment
    B. Dems wrong: gvt nds "hmn cap" infrastructure.

Next, if you haven't thought of the convenient set of symbols provided by 200 years of political cartoons as the fodder for making this speech more memorable to you, then you've missed the boat!

Here is a great set of symbols to build your chain link around so that you can remember the speech above:

Democrats = Donkeys
Republicans = Elephants
Government = Uncle Sam
Rich = The tycoon from the game of Monopoly

Based on these convenient pictographs, here's what your chain link might be like:

I.   An elephant wielding an ax in its trunk (the tax cut) rides along with a tycoon on his back.
      A. The tycoon shakes hands with Ronald Reagan and begins throwing gifts and money down to a crowd.
      B. Bush jumps on the elephant and the tycoon jumps for joy. The elephant swings an ax through a tree labeled, "capital gains tax."
II.   The tycoon gets off the elephant. A donkey picks his pocket and throws the money to a crowd of poor folks.
III. The elephant and donkey arm wrestle, while a balloon, labeled, "Budget", flies above them.
IV.   The elephant and donkey sit in a classroom being lectured by a professor and looking crestfallen.

Get the picture?

The whole key to good memory is establishing tags, links, associations—anything that will help your mind reel the memories in from the deep abyss of your memory banks.

The point of this chapter and all of the others within this book is to show you how simple this can be. But the rest is up to you. Developing a good memory requires you to practice the techniques I've discussed throughout this book.

After you've done so, you'll be more likely to get higher grades on exams that test your knowledge of facts. What's more, you might never forget where your keys, wallet or glasses are again.

I'd advise you to go back and read through Chapters 3 through 9 again, make conscious use of the techniques and then take the test in Chapter 11. If you do your homework, you'll probably score high.

Good luck!

Chapter Eleven

LET'S NOT FORGET ADD

We both fear and pity kids on illegal drugs. But we also must face and deal with what's happening to the 3 million-plus who are on a *legal* drug—Ritalin, the prescribed drug of choice for kids diagnosed with Attention Deficit Disorder (ADD), hyperactivity or the combination of the two (ADHD).

I could write a book on ADD, which seems to be the "diagnosis of choice" for school kids these days. Luckily, I don't have to. Thom Hartmann has already written an excellent one—*Attention Deficit Disorder: A Different Perception*—from which I have freely and liberally borrowed (with his permission) for this chapter.

I'm going to leave others to debate whether ADD actually exists as a clearly definable illness, whether it's the "catchall" diagnosis of lazy doctors, whether teachers are labeling kids as ADD to avoid taking responsibility for the students' poor learning skills, whether Ritalin is a miracle drug or one that is medicating creative kids into a conforming stupor.

All of these positions *have* been asserted, and, as hundreds of new kids are medicated every day, the debate about ADD is only likely to continue...and heat up.

That is not my concern in this book.

What I want to deal with here is the reality that many kids, however they're labeled, have severe problems in dealing with school as it usually exists. And to give them the advice they need—especially regarding methods to remember more of what they read and study—to contend with the symptoms that have acquired the label "ADD".

Some definitions, please

Just what is ADD? It's probably easiest to describe as a person's difficulty focusing on a simple thing for any significant period of time. People with ADD are described as easily distracted, impatient, impulsive and often seeking immediate gratitude. They often have poor listening skills and have trouble doing "boring" jobs (like sitting quietly in class or, as adults, balancing a checkbook). "Disorganized" and "messy" are words that also come up a lot.

Hyperactivity, on the other hand, is more clearly defined as restlessness, resulting in excessive activity. Hyperactives are usually described as having "ants in their pants." ADHD, the first category recognized in medicine some 75 years ago, is a combination of hyperactivity and ADD.)

According to the American Psychiatric Association, a person has ADHD if they meet eight or more of the following paraphrased criteria:

1. They can't remain seated if required to do so.

2. They are easily distracted by extraneous stimuli.

3. Focusing on a single task or play activity is difficult.

4. Frequently begin another activity without completing the first.

5. Fidgets or squirms (or feels restless mentally).

6. Can't (or doesn't want to) wait for his turn during group activities

7. Will often interrupt with an answer before a question is completed.

8. Has problems with chore or job follow-through

9. Can't play quietly easily.

10. Impulsively jumps into physically dangerous activities without weighing the consequences.

11. Easily loses things (pencils, tools, papers) necessary to complete school or work projects

12. Interrupts others inappropriately.

13. Talks impulsively or excessively.

14. Doesn't seem to listen when spoken to.

Three caveats to keep in mind: The behaviors must have started before age seven, not represent some other form of classifiable mental illness and occur more frequently than the average person of the same age.

Characteristics of people with ADD

Let's look at the characteristics generally ascribed to people with ADD in more detail:

Easily distracted—Since ADD people are constantly "scoping out" everything around them, focusing on a single item is difficult. Just try having a conversation with an ADD person while a television is on.

Short, but very intense, attention span—Though it can't be defined in terms of minutes or hours, anything an ADD person finds boring immediately loses their attention. Other projects may hold their rapt and extraordinarily intense attention for hours or days. Needless to say, this affects memory since, as we've discussed, it's virtually impossible to remember something in which you have absolutely no interest!

Disorganization—ADD children and adults are often chronically disorganized—their rooms are messy, their desk a shambles, their files incoherent. While people without ADD can certainly be equally messy and disorganized, they can usually find what they are looking for; ADDers *can't*.

Distortions of time-sense—ADDers have an exaggerated sense of urgency when they're working on something and an exaggerated sense of boredom when they have nothing interesting to do.

Difficulty following directions—A new theory on this aspect holds that ADDers have difficulty processing auditory or verbal information. A significant aspect of this difficulty is the very-common reports of parents of ADD kids who say their kids love to watch TV and hate to read.

Daydream—Or fall into depressions or mood-swings.

Take risks—ADDers seem to make faster decisions than non-ADDers. Which is why Thom Hartmann and Wilson Harrell, former publisher of *Inc.* magazine and author of ***For Entrepreneurs Only***, conclude that the vast majority of successful entrepreneurs probably have ADD! They call them "Hunters", as opposed to the more staid "Farmer" types.

Easily frustrated and impatient—ADDers do *not* beat around the bush or suffer fools gladly. They are direct and to-the-point. When things aren't working, "Do something!" is the ADD rallying cry, even if that something is a bad idea.

Why ADD kids have trouble in school

First and foremost, says Thom Hartmann, it's because schools are set up for "Farmers"—sit at a desk, do what you're told, watch and listen to the teacher. This is pure hell for the "Hunters" with ADD. The bigger the class size, the worse it becomes. Kids with ADD, remember, are easily distracted, easily bored, easily turned off, always ready to move on.

What should you look for in a school setting to make it more palatable to an ADD son or daughter? What can you do at home to help your child (or yourself)? Hartmann has some solid answers:

- *Learning needs to be project- and experience-based*, providing more opportunities for creativity and shorter and smaller "bites" of information. Many "gifted" programs offer exactly such opportunities. The problem for many kids with ADD is that they've spent years in non-gifted, Farmer-type classroom settings and may be labeled underachieving behavior problems, effectively shut out of the programs virtually designed for them! Many parents report that children diagnosed as ADD, who failed miserably in public school, thrived in private school. Hartmann attributes this to the smaller classrooms, more individual attention with specific goal-setting, project-based learning and similar methods common in such schools. These factors are just what make ADD kids thrive!

- ***Create a weekly performance template*** on which *both* teacher and parent chart the child's performance, positive and negative. "Creating such a larger-than-the-child system," claims Hartmann, "will help keep ADD children on task and on time."

- ***Encourage special projects for extra credit.*** Projects give ADDers the chance to learn in the mode that's most appropriate to them. They will also give such kids the chance to make up for the "boring" homework they sometimes simply can't make themselves do.

- ***Stop labeling them "disordered"***—Kids react to labels, especially negative ones, even more than adults. Saying "you have a deficit and a disorder" may be more destructive than useful.

- ***Think twice about medication,*** but don't discard it as an option. Hartmann has a very real concern about the long-term side effects of the drugs normally prescribed for ADDers. He also notes that they may well be more at risk to be substance abusers as adults, so starting them on medication at a young age sends a very mixed message. On the other hand, if an ADD child cannot have his or her special needs met in the classroom, *not* medicating him or her may be a disaster. "The relatively unknown long-term risks of drug therapy," says Hartmann, "may be more than offset by the short-term benefits of improved classroom performance."

Specific suggestions about improving your memory

- ***Practice, practice, practice*** all the memory techniques detailed in this book. As we've previously noted,

ADDers tend to have trouble listening and are easily distracted. As a result, they may fail to remember things they simply never heard or paid attention to. Work specifically on the various visualization techniques discussed. Practice making mental pictures of things when having conversations; create mental images of your "to do" list; visualize doing things to which you've committed or for which you are receiving instructions or directions. And, of course, practice careful listening skills. Many of Harry Lorayne's memory books (especially his classic, *The Memory Book*), which stress many "picture-oriented" approaches to memory problems, should be considered invaluable additions to any ADDer's library.

- *Write* **everything** *down*. This is something I recommend everyone doing, but it is absolutely essential for ADDers. The more you write down, the less you have to remember!

- Rather than attempting to take notes using words—even the abbreviations and shorthand I've recommended in *Take Notes*—ADDers should instead *utilize pictures, mapping, diagrams, etc.* in lieu of outlines or "word" notes.

- Despite what I wrote in *How to Study*, *ADDers should tape record lectures*. This will enable them to relisten and reprocess information they may have missed the first time around.

- *Create distraction-free zones.* Henry David Thoreau (who evidently suffered from ADD, by the way) was so desperate to escape distraction he moved to isolated Walden Pond. Organize your time and workspace to create your own "Walden Pond", especially when you have to write, take notes, read or study. ADDers need silence, so consider the library. Another tip: Clean your work area thoroughly at the end of each day. This will minimize distractions.

• ***Train your attention span.*** ADDers will probably never be able to train themselves to ignore distractions totally, but a variety of meditation techniques might help them stay focused longer.

Chapter Twelve

TEST YOUR NEW MEMORY POWER

As promised, I'm going to give you a chance to check your progress. If you've studied the contents of this book thoroughly and have made an effort to put some of its advice to work, you should score much higher now than you did on the quiz in Chapter 2.

Test #1: The mnemonic alphabet

Study the number below for 30 seconds. Then cover it up and replicate as much as you can, taking only another 20 seconds or so.

48850291641023486423

Test #2: A better vocabulary

Here are some relatively obscure vocabulary words and their meanings. Study them for no more than three minutes, then answer the questions below.

Grigri: An African charm

Frowsty: Musty or ill-smelling.

Electrophorous: An instrument for generating static electricity.

Baedeker: A travel guidebook.

Expurgate: To amend by removing words or passages

Pidgin: A simplified form of English or another language, incorporating elements of the local language(s).

Dvandva: A compound word in which neither element is subordinate to the other (example: *bittersweet*).

Patois: A dialect of a language.

Marsupium: The pouch on the abdomen of a female marsupial (e.g., a kangaroo)

Patrimony: Property inherited from one's father.

Baksheesh: A small gift of money.

Captious: Fond of finding fault or raising objections about trivial things.

Kachina: Various ancestral spirits deified by the Hopi Indians.

Heriot: A feudal service or tribute.

Portmanteau: A trunk for clothes.

Improve Your Memory

Gustatory Of or pertaining to taste.

Malleable: Able to be hammered or pressed into shape.

Torpor: A condition of sluggishness/inactivity.

Bumptious: Conceited.

Dolerite: A coarse-grained variety of basalt.

Okay, cover them up and take this test:

Someone who is sluggish is in a _____.

Something is "malleable" if it can be _____.

A baksheesh is a small gift of _____.

Someone who is constantly finding fault with others can be said to be _____.

When cultures blend, the resulting language is known as _____.

Inheritance from one's father is: _____

A large trunk for clothes is a _____.

He referred to his _____ while travelling.

A bumptious person is A) humble or B) stuck up?

A patois of English is _____.

A beautiful Nigerian necklace could be a _____.

The baby wombat slept in its mother's _____.

"Gosh, Jeeves, that tuxedo is pretty _____.

Ben Franklin, *sans* kite, could have used an _____.

The publisher maintained that his edition of Ulysses was

_____.

Dvandva means _____.

Hopi ancestral spirits are called _____.

When the serf died, a _____ was due his lord.

Where might you have a gustatory experience? _____

The miners were looking for gold but found_____.

Test #3: Dates & events

Study the following dates, events and facts. Then take the test on the next page.

Jamestown, the first permanent European settlement in the New World, was founded in 1607.

The Korean War, though never officially declared, raged from 1950 to 1953.

Pilgrims signed the Mayflower Compact in 1620.

Thomas Jefferson purchased the Louisiana Territory from Napoleon in 1803.

1967: London Bridge is moved to Arizona

Eli Whitney invented the cotton gin in 1793.

The population of California is 23,668,000

Harvard, oldest university in the U.S., was founded in 1636.

With an annual rainfall of 3.73 inches, Nevada is the driest state in the Union.

Improve Your Memory

President McKinley was assassinated in 1901.

Congress passed the Tonkin Gulf Resolution, increasing American involvement in the Vietnam War in 1964.

George Washington was inaugurated in New York City in 1789.

The horrific battle of Gettysburg was fought in 1863.

30,000 people work in the Pentagon building.

1850: California is admitted to the union as a state

1876: Alexander Graham Bell invents the telephone

Now answer the following questions:

1. The cotton gin was invented when and by whom?
2. The Battle of Gettysburg raged in what year?
3. How many people live in California?
4. In what year was Jamestown founded?
5. How many inches of rain fall on the driest state of the Union? What state is it?
6. What is the name and founding date of the oldest university in the United States?
7. True or false: George Washington was inaugurated in Philadelphia. In what year did it occur?
8. When and by whom was the telephone invented?
9. When and to what state was the London Bridge moved?
10. How many people work in the Pentagon?
11. When did America enter into full-scale conflict in Vietnam?

12. When did Teddy Roosevelt succeed McKinley?

13. America became the proud owner of New Orleans in what year?

14. When did the Korean War take place.

15. When did the Pilgrims sign the Mayflower Compact?

Test #4: Reading retention

Scan the following three paragraphs in order to answer the questions that follow (which you may read first). This should take you no more than two minutes.

When told to communicate, most people immediately think of writing or speaking—verbal communication. Yet, there is another form of communication that everyone uses, often without realizing it. Through various facial expressions, body movements and gestures, we all have a system of nonverbal communication.

We constantly signal to others our feelings and attitudes unconsciously through actions we may not even realize we are performing. One type is called *barrier signals*. Since most people usually feel safer behind a barrier, they often unthinkingly fold their arms or find some other pretext for placing their arms in front of their body when they feel insecure.

Such nonverbal communication can lead to serious misunderstanding if you are not careful. Take the simple symbol you make by forming a circle with your thumb and forefinger. In

America it means "OK", but in France, it signifies a zero, something—or someone—of no
value. Imagine the offense a French waiter might
take if you signified your satisfaction with your
meal with this sign! You would offend and insult, when you intended only praise.

1. Communicating through body signals is often:

   A. Nonverbal

   B. Conscious

   C. Unconscious

   D. Unnoticeable

2. Through facial expressions and body movements, we
   communicate:

   A. Attitudes and emotions

   B. Facts and figures

   C. Praise or insults

   D. Friendships

3. People fold their arms when they feel:

   A. Insecure

   B. Disillusioned

   C. Depressed

   D. Ecstatic

4. The thumb-forefinger symbol is an insult to:

   A. Waiters

   B. Americans

   C. Everyone

   D. The French

Now *read* the following passage and answer the questions that follow (but do *not* look at the questions first). Give yourself four minutes for this exercise:

Mabel Dodge Luhan had an extraordinary effect on the life of the little mountain town of Taos, New Mexico. From the time she arrived in 1917 until her death in 1962, Mabel was the social and cultural life of the town. She not only brought her own personality to the artists' colony, but numerous artists and writers to visit Taos as well. Some of them remained in the area for the rest of their lives.

The gatherings of these famous people— D.H. Lawrence, Georgia O'Keeffe, Greta Garbo, Leopold Stokowski and others—in Mabel's house served as a kind of "salon" where important members of the American and European artistic communities met, discussed each other's work, and spread the word about Taos and Mabel when they returned to New York, California or Europe. Their enthusiasm helped bring even more famous people to visit Taos.

The social scene in Taos centered on Mabel. Because she was a personal friend of most of the people who visited her, as well as being wealthy, domineering and extremely active, she reigned as the head of the social order in the town during her entire lifetime. The other prominent members of the community—the artists, the wealthy ranchers, the merchants—all formed a pecking order beneath her.

Mabel's support of the artistic community earlier in this century helped spread the fame of these artists—and increased the sale of their works. The prominence of Taos as an artists' colony, thanks in part to Mabel, encouraged even more artists to move to Taos, which, in turn, increased the number of visitors who came to town to buy art or simply to look at it—while spending money at the restaurants, hotels, bars and gift shops. This trend has continued—Taos today is a major art center in the U.S. with dozens of art galleries and tourist-related shops.

The historic, as well as artistic, aspects of Taos were promoted by Mabel. Her artist friends painted people, places and events connected to the local Spanish and Native American cultures. These paintings, and the media attention given to the historic aspects of the town, helped spread the fame of Taos.

Today, Mabel's house and her grave, in the historic Kit Carson Cemetery, are two of many attractions that tourists visit when they come to town.

It is difficult to imagine what Taos would be like today had Mabel Dodge Luhan not taken up residence there in 1917. Her promotion of the little town for so many years gave it worldwide fame. Artists, historians, writers and tourists began to visit Taos. Each year, the number of visitors—and social and cultural events, art galleries and historic tours—increases, thanks to the ongoing influence of Mabel Dodge Luhan.

1. How many years did Mabel live in Taos?
2. Where is Mabel buried?
3. Name three famous people Mabel lured to Taos.

Test #5: Remembering lists, no matter how obscure

Study the first two lists for one minute each, then close the book and recite them back. Do the same for the third and fourth lists, except allow three minutes for the third, five minutes for the fourth:

Wine-bottle sizes: Baby, balthasar, jeroboam, magnum, Methuselah, nebuchadnezzar, nip, rehoboam, Salmanazar

Jewish calendar: Ab, Abib, Adar, Adar Sheni, Elul, Hes(h)van, Iy(y)ar, Kislev, Nisan, S(h)ebat, Sivan, Tammuz, Tebet(h), Tis(h)ri, Veadar.

Selected Parliaments: Althing (Iceland), Cortes (Spain, Portugal), ecclesia (Athens), Knesset (Israel), Lagting (Norway), Majlis (Iran), Rigsdag (Denmark), Seanad (Ireland), Skupshtina (Yugoslavia), Tynwald (Isle of Man).

Cattle breeds: Aficander, Alderney, Angus, Ankole, Ayrshire, Blonde d'Aquitaine, Brahman, Brown Swiss, cattabu, cattalo, Charol(l)ais, Chillingham, Devon, dexter, Durham, Friesian, Galloway, Guernsey, Hereford, Highland, Holstein, Jersey, Latvian, Limousin, Luing, Red Poll, Romagnola, Santa Gertrudis, short-horn, Simmenthaler, Teeswater, Ukrainian, Welsh Black.

Test #6: Remembering the rules of English spelling

Identify the misspelled words in the following list:

Immediatly

Stoney

Likeable

Judgement

Measurement

Recieve

Liesure

Commited

Occurence

Compeling

Disatisfied

Harrasment

Embarassment

Drunkeness

Unconvincible

Regretible

Mistake

Mistatement

How did you do? (See the bottom of this page for the spelling solutions.)

I hope that you scored well and are confident that you can approach your schoolwork—and the rest of your life, inside and outside of school—with the assurance that your memory will be an ally rather than a foil.

In the above list, the following are the only words spelled correctly: stoney (though stony is preferred), likeable, mistake, unconvincible and measurement.

INDEX